SELF-PUBLISHING FOR NEW AUTHORS

DALE L. ROBERTS

Self-Publishing for New Authors: A Guide for Writing and Publishing Your First Book

By Dale L. Roberts

©2024 One Jacked Monkey, LLC

eBook ISBN: 978-1-63925-033-2
Paperback ISBN: 978-1-63925-034-9
Hardcover ISBN: 978-1-63925-035-6
Audiobook ISBN: 978-1-63925-036-3

All rights reserved. No part of this book may be reproduced in any form by any electronic or mechanical means, including information storage and retrieval systems, without permission in writing from the copyright owner, except by a reviewer who may quote brief passages in a review.

Some recommended links in this book are part of affiliate programs. This means if you purchase a product through one of the links, then I get a portion of each sale. It doesn't affect your cost and helps support the cause. If you have any reservations about buying a product through my affiliate link, then Google a direct link and bypass the affiliate link.

CONTENTS

FOREWORD 1

INTRODUCTION 4

SECTION 1: WRITE 7

SECTION 2: EDIT 34

SECTION 3: FORMAT 47

SECTION 4: PUBLISH 62

SECTION 5: THE HIDDEN COSTS OF SELF-PUBLISHING 125

CONCLUSION 150

GET MORE BOOK SALES TODAY! 153

A SMALL ASK 155

ABOUT THE AUTHOR 156

SPECIAL THANKS 157

ADDITIONAL RESOURCES 158

REFERENCES 161

GET MY BESTSELLER BOOK LAUNCH CHECKLIST ABSOLUTELY FREE!

Want to launch your book to bestseller status on Amazon? Sign up for my email newsletter today and get my **Bestseller Book Launch Checklist** for FREE! This step-by-step plan will help you make your book a hit.

But that's not all! When you subscribe, you'll also get my email newsletter packed with the latest self-publishing news and tips. Get all you need to know in just one or two emails per week.

Subscribe now and grab your free checklist at
DaleLinks.com/Checklist

"I've used dozens of book cover design services over the last ten years, and none compare to the level of quality and professionalism that Miblart delivers."

— *Dale L. Roberts* —

Miblart - a book cover design company for self-published authors

Designers who specialize in different genres	Unlimited number of revisions
No deposit to get started	You can pay in installments

GET A BOOK COVER THAT WILL BECOME YOUR N°1 MARKETING TOOL

Excellent

   4.9

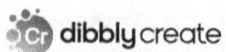

UnBlock Writers Block

Trouble Finishing Your Book? Or Even Starting?

Meet **Dibbly Create.** Your All-in-1 A.I. companion for publishing your book

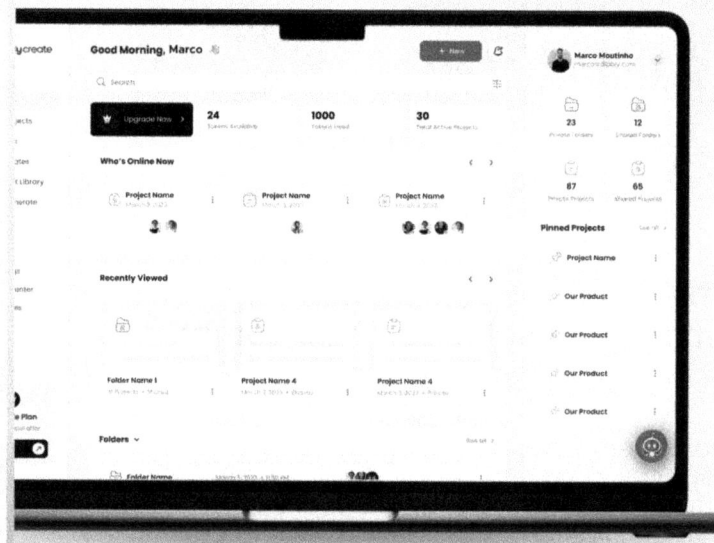

With Dibbly, it's done.

- ✓ Research
- ✓ Writing
- ✓ Editing
- ✓ Formatting
- ✓ Proofreading
- ✓ Designing
- ✓ Publish-Ready

Yes, I Need Help Finishing my Book

Try for Free!
Scan the QR Code or visit   dibbly.com/create

Next level tools to help you grow.

Whether you're an aspiring author or international bestseller, we've got the tools to help you publish faster, distribute wider and manage your business easier.

Learn more by going to **d2d.tips/dale** and read on to discover some of what sets D2D apart:

- ✓ **Automated end-matter**
- ✓ **New Release Notifications for readers**
- ✓ **Payment Splitting for contributors**
- ✓ **Scheduled price changes**
- ✓ **Smashwords store coupons**
- ✓ **Universal Book Links via Books2Read.com**

It's print-on-demand reimagined.

Create a paperback on draft2digital.com from your existing ebook with just a few clicks, and **create a full, wrap-around book cover from your ebook cover**. It really is that easy!

Massive annual sales, self-serve promotion tools, and the **industry's best royalty rates** of up to 80% list. Readers love discovering breakout indie authors at smashwords.com.

Win **awards** and get **reviews** for **your book**

25% off your first purchase

bookawardpro.com

FOREWORD

I hate forewords in books! I mean, you picked up a book by Dale L. Roberts, and here you are, reading a couple of pages from some joker you probably don't know. Here's the thing: you and I aren't that different. It wasn't long ago I decided to take the plunge and self-publish my own book. I won't lie; introducing my written baby to the world was scary. But I did it. Fast forward three years, and I'd made a decent little side business for myself. Nothing earth-shattering, but enough to help make daily life a bit less stressful financially. Then I met Dale L. Roberts!

Do you like YouTube? I love YouTube! When I started my self-publishing business, I watched hours of YouTube videos on how to self-publish. There was only one problem: I was getting mixed messages. One "guru" would tell me to do this, then another "expert" would say the opposite. What was true, and what was hogwash? Here was the issue: many of these so-called "gurus" were spouting all this advice based on publishing they'd done years ago. This probably won't come as a surprise to you, but things change. If these guys and gals weren't still publishing books, how could I trust they knew what would work now?

The fact that you're holding Dale's book shows he knows what he's talking about. He walks the walk and continues to publish books today. After I stumbled upon his YouTube channel and saw his passion for publishing, I knew this guy was for real. I soon joined his coaching program, and he showed me what I was doing right and where I could make some changes. Between his passion for the industry and his ability to motivate, my drive to make this self-publishing thing take off exploded. After implementing his tips, I was able to *triple* my self-publishing business. That wasn't enough for Dale. He also challenged me to start my own YouTube channel. I did, and now, two years later, *Keith Wheeler Books* has over twenty thousand subscribers. I'm telling you, Dale's motivational talks are no joke!

Self-Publishing for New Authors is the book I wish I had five years ago when I first started. By picking up this book, you've given yourself one of the greatest gifts: a how-to guide that will streamline the learning process. While there aren't guarantees in self-publishing, as in life, you've greatly increased your chance for success by arming yourself with the most actionable tool to minimize the learning curve. This guide will have you complete "publishing a book" on your to-do list.

So, how do you get there? First and foremost, read this book. The laundry can wait. It'll still be there later. Second, as you work your way through the book, take action! The knowledge in the following chapters will do you no good if you don't put it into practice. Third, even when you're done with this book, be sure to keep it someplace handy because you'll most likely refer to it even after you've published your first book. Last but certainly not least, leave an honest review on Amazon for this book. As you may or may not already know, reviews are the best way to thank an author for the work they've done. Since getting reviews will be a huge goal for your books, why not appease the review gods by leaving one yourself? It'll give you that nice, warm, fuzzy feeling inside.

Anyway, I wish you the best of luck as you begin this exciting journey into self-publishing. I know you're in great hands!

Okay, enough of this foreword crap. Let's get to the good stuff!

Keith Wheeler

Award-Winning Author & Host of *Keith Wheeler Books* on YouTube

INTRODUCTION

Everyone has a unique story to share about their entry point into the business of self-publishing. My story started around early 2014 when I finished writing my first book about health and wellness. Though I'd shared what I was doing with my wife, Kelli, she never expected it to go beyond a mere hobby. Every morning for over a year, I got up in the wee hours to churn out my first manuscript before she got out of bed. This allowed me uninterrupted time to peck away at the keyboard and produce a full-length book that I could be proud of.

So you can imagine her surprise when I told her I was planning to self-publish my manuscript through a local print shop. The cost? $1,200!

You'd think it would have taken Kelli a few minutes to process a response, but not her. She seemed to have a ready-made answer to any issues regarding money. Deep down, we both knew the $1,200 was merely the start of things to come. After all, if the cost was $1,200, what was next? Would it escalate to $2,400? Or could it get even worse and grow to $10,000?

"Where are you going to get that money?" she asked.

INTRODUCTION

Less than two years earlier, we'd been struggling to make ends meet. In fact, I had to donate plasma just to get a few bucks to put food on our table. Now that we were in the clear, I was looking to sacrifice our financial comfort for this passion project.

Though my end goal was to write a book and share the soft copy with friends and family, I soon came to realize that more people needed to see it. I wanted more of the world to benefit from my months of labor. Like a father, I beamed with pride over my creation: a 44,000-word manuscript.

Despite knowing this investment should have been a joint decision, I visited a local printer to see how much it would run me. The cost might have been more, and I'm not entirely sure how many print copies I got for the investment. The biggest issue was that I'd tried wagering a bet with our money without my wife's consent.

Many aspiring authors face this problem. We're so anxious to share our work with the world that we'd do it at the expense of our livelihood, lifestyle, and even relationships. But it doesn't have to be that way.

When you want to share your message with the world, self-publishing is one practical solution to consider. In years past, most people viewed self-publishing as an inferior path or something only failed authors did. Not anymore! Mark Dawson and Hugh Howey, known for their success in traditional publishing, switched to self-publishing. Why?

Contemporary self-publishing is more accessible and workable than ever. You don't have to invest $1,200 on a pallet of books that will collect dust in your garage for years to come. You can spend as much or as little as you'd like. It's all up to you. That's the sweet part about self-publishing—you're in charge! No one can tell you what to do.

With little more than time and sweat equity, you can have a beautiful product. Authors now have more opportunities thanks to print on demand, ebooks, and downloadable audiobooks. All it takes is a little up-front work and a little resourcefulness.

Back in 2013, I didn't know much about self-publishing. I knew there had been an explosion of ebooks, but I didn't see the viability of digital publishing. I simply wanted to publish my manuscript as a paperback. Heck, I never even thought about audiobooks at that point. That didn't seem achievable since I believed I'd have to hire professional narrators and book a studio to record it in. I had so many misconceptions back then! If I could go back in time and set myself straight, I would save my past self a lot of heartache.

Self-Publishing for New Authors is my attempt to pull together the most valuable lessons I wish I could share with my past self—information that's perfect for newcomers to self-publishing. Maybe you had a spouse who shot you down when you asked for money to publish a book. Perhaps you're someone who questions their publishing skills, despite having the passion and talent for writing.

In the coming chapters, we're going to clear up confusion about self-publishing your book. As part of that, I'll give you the best first steps to getting it all done, including touching on some advice for writing the book. It's hard to publish a book without spending money, but I'll explain the potential costs and ways to reduce them without compromising quality.

By the last page, you'll have a better understanding of where to go with your book and what to do. When sharing a wild idea with your partner, you'll be better prepared to answer questions. Let's dig in and get started on your self-publishing journey.

SECTION 1: WRITE

To be clear, I will not teach you how to write in this section. Learning how to write deserves more specialized insights from writing experts. Everyone can agree that you can't become a talented writer if you don't write. Much like an artist cannot perfect their craft without sketching and a bricklayer cannot build better houses without laying bricks, it takes time and practice to hone your craft. Be okay with where you are as a writer and adjust as you go.

Before you ever put pen to paper or hit your first keystroke, you must lay the groundwork for your manuscript. It's a practice that has helped me publish dozens of books and a process that will serve as a better workflow for you.

RESEARCH BEFORE YOU WRITE

The biggest mistake I made when I wrote my first book was this: I did it to scratch an itch. Though it's admirable to tackle such a large project with no real purpose, your outcome will vary. If you are anything like I was, then go for it. You can skip researching altogether, but you're limiting who you can reach and what you can accomplish with your book after publishing. If you're simply writing for the love of the craft, then kudos to you.

When you're ready to see the bigger picture, start by asking **who** will read your book. No, your mom doesn't count. Your next-door neighbor's best friend isn't any better. Be more specific about who your ideal reader is.

Even before you flesh out any ideas or concepts, know with whom you're having a conversation. For instance, you wouldn't walk into a crowded party and start talking to no one in particular. You would most likely scan the room for a familiar or friendly face to strike up a conversation. The same is true for your book. Dial in who you're writing for and why they should care.

Use some scrap paper and jot down answers to these questions:

1. How old is your reader?
2. What is your reader's education level?
3. What interests your reader most?
4. What will your book say that is worthy of your reader's attention?
5. How can you keep your reader's attention for the entirety of your book?
6. What is your reader's problem, and do you have the solution?

Some experts have you identify how your reader looks, how they interact with others, what they write, and when they read. That's fine, but you don't need everything down to the fingerprint of your ideal reader. You just need to have a rough understanding of who will read your content.

Have you ever noticed how you speak to babies? Do you use baby talk and make a fool of yourself? Take the way you speak to a baby and imagine doing it with a mature adult. How do you think they'll react? I'm sure they'd assume you're out of your mind.

Though it's an extreme case, how you speak to a baby versus an adult clearly illustrates why you have to know who your audience is. Romance readers expect something very different from thriller readers. If you want to sell books, you can write romance in your thriller or a thrilling romance, but understanding what the reader wants from your book will help you sell to the right audience.

Don't make the mistake most people do thinking that your writing might appeal to everyone. If you want to self-publish, yes, you can write what you want, but the publishing side will require you to think like a publisher. And that starts with understanding who your reader is—and by reader we mean customer—and what they expect to find in your book.

Much like I shared in *Amazon Keywords for Books*:

"When you write for everyone, you write for no one."

Adults don't want you to speak to them like babies, and babies won't understand what you're communicating if you talk to them like adults. In the same way, write what best fits the conversation. The better you identify your ideal reader, the better you communicate.

Don't expect to get this right on your first book. Heck, it might take multiple efforts to figure out the creative side. Starting with understanding who will read your book will help you more effectively write that book.

Once you have your ideal reader in mind, is it time to write? Well, not just yet.

You need proof of concept first. There's nothing worse than writing for an audience of none. Dig a little deeper to see who your audience is and what they expect in your writing.

DEEPER RESEARCH WRITING

While having your ideal reader in mind is helpful for writing, do you really know who they are and what they expect from you? Rather than assume, let's remove as much ambiguity as possible before you even type the first word. It all begins with a little reconnaissance, gathering all the info you need to deliver the goods better.

You can start your research at a local library or bookstore. To make matters a little easier and more accessible, I highly recommend using the internet for most of your research. The biggest issue with researching in-store or at the library is that you won't truly appreciate the global demand for books within specific topics or niches. When you use online search engines, you have nearly precise answers to what you're looking for in your ideal reader.

A few places to research include these search engines:

- Amazon
- Google
- YouTube

You can also research other platforms more specific to books, like Barnes & Noble or Kobo. For now, let's keep you on the path of least resistance by using the three resources with the most traffic and arguably the best results.

Each of these three platforms has a unique search engine algorithm, which is a complex mathematical formula based on consumer behaviors. The more consumers use a search engine, the more the algorithm adjusts to accommodate future queries better.

Have you ever noticed the prepopulated list of recommendations when you type into a search engine? Also known as auto-complete, this list of words and phrases represents the popular search queries based on what you're currently typing. As you type out one word, the search engine tries to guess what you're searching for. The words or phrases that auto-complete are keywords.

Auto-completed keywords are the best predictors of what consumers search for online.

A huge reason you want to use Amazon, Google, and YouTube for research is to see what the public searches. Once you get a good idea about what they're searching for, you can have an even better idea of your direction in writing.

You're not going to simply rely on auto-complete to do all your research for writing. It's going to require a deeper, more granular approach. Keywords alone won't help guide you in the right direction. The search results and consumer demand play a huge part in what has proof of concept and what isn't worth a dime.

WHAT TO LOOK FOR IN RESEARCH

You'll know whether a topic is worth pursuing based on articles, blog posts, and videos. For instance, when searching for "how to work out at home," you may find several videos on YouTube about it. If the average number of views is around 100,000 among all the videos, chances are pretty likely you have found a winning topic to cover. You can search for the same topic and find a host of online articles, but the problem is knowing how many people read those posts. Sure, you can use many online programs to estimate traffic on the article, but that becomes way too complex.

Let's keep it simple. After YouTube and Google, you can stick with Amazon to measure proof of concept. You'll find the metrics much easier to see and make better-informed decisions based on your research. Discerning between useful and inessential information is possibly the hardest part. The essential items and metrics to focus on begin with the keywords.

In *Amazon Keywords for Books*, I share the complexities of keywords and how they function. Here's the best summary of how keywords function:

Keywords are the shared interests people have and the way for people to identify with other people. Without keywords, online users would mindlessly scroll through websites, trying to find their topic of interest.

What exactly are keywords? They're a single word or string of words in a phrase describing what a consumer searches online. It should be noted that a keyword isn't simply a single word all the time. Keywords describe a specific search query or are identifiers of varied results.

Where most authors get keywords wrong is defining this in a very narrow way. For example, if you're a fitness writer, you may want to write about exercise. Rather than relying on just one term, here are a few examples of keywords that might be helpful to your research:

1. Workout
2. Home workouts
3. At-home workouts for women
4. Workouts for women over 55
5. Chair workout

With fiction, you'll see similarities as well:

1. Horror
2. Horror books for adults
3. Horror anthology
4. Sci-fi horror novels
5. Military sci-fi horror

Let's take a deeper look at the keywords worth pursuing and break down key indicators of the best selections.

KEYWORD RESEARCH

To get the best results, open your browser in incognito mode. Using an incognito browser will give you the purest results because no queries will be served to you based on your earlier experience. When using a regular browser, you're allowing search engines to use your previous browsing history to deliver the best results suited to your needs. You don't want to know what is good for *you* but what is good for the general population.

The most popular results will help you tailor your writing to the current consumer demands. If you want to make a decent living from your work, tune into what is in demand. As a new author, you won't have to sell your soul or compromise your writing, but you will need to meet your readers in the middle.

Visit Amazon through an incognito browser. Click the **All** drop-down menu to the left of the search box, then change the category drop-down to **Books** or **Kindle Store**. Now, think about what you're most interested in writing. Begin typing a word or phrase associated with the writing topic. Do not press **Enter**. Allow auto-complete to serve a drop-down list of recommendations.

Write down all relevant keywords. Don't worry about keywords unrelated to your potential writing. Once you complete writing one list, try another word or phrase in the search box. Then, repeat the process. Once you think you've exhausted all possibilities, try the keyword alphabet research method. Type in your first word or phrase and add a space after it. Now, type in the letter **A** and make a note of any relevant keywords. Once you note all relevant options, hit backspace and type in **B**. After writing those options, continue through the rest of the alphabet.

As you go along, you'll notice longer keyword phrases of about three or more words. Also known as long-tail keywords, these keyword types are where you'll find the most success. For one, you get a better idea of what people want.

As an example, most anyone will search "workout." While "workout" can be a popular search, it is incredibly broad and doesn't accurately describe who is searching for it. When you type in "workouts for women over 55," you'll notice it narrows down the search to who and what they want. If a woman is over fifty-five years old and looking for a workout, then chances are pretty likely they'll use a long-tail keyword.

When you have about twenty-four or more good long-tail keywords in your list, do a little more focused research. Grab a keyword, type it into the search box, and hit **Enter** for the results.

First, focus on the number of products showing on the first-page search by looking at the top left of the website. You'll see the first sixteen products or fewer. Next to the number of products on the first page are the total products associated with that keyword.

You'll see something like the following:

1–16 of over 1,000 results for "workouts for women over 55"

The more products associated with a keyword, the more competitive you can assume it is to get any attention. When you can find a lower number of products, it's safe to assume your future book has a greater potential for discovery. However, if you find that few products appear in a keyword search, the product may not be in demand.

The best range of products associated with a keyword should be above one hundred but below ten thousand. With those numbers in mind, eliminate keywords outside of that range.

ANALYZE THE BOOKS

Once you complete a search, scroll through the first sixteen options. Ignore any product with the word "Sponsored" at the top. Those are ads and are not relevant to your research. Instead, focus on the sixteen other books in the main column. Now, select a book and visit the product page.

On the product page, you'll be most concerned with how well the product sells. Scroll down to the **Product details** section below the description. You'll see all the pertinent information about the book. The part you should focus on is the overall Amazon Best Sellers Rank

(ABSR). This rank is how well the product sells compared to other products in the Amazon marketplace. The closer the product ranks to #1, the better. The farther away from the #1 spot, the worse off. If the product has no ABSR, it hasn't sold a single copy.

Write the overall ABSR of the book, then go back one page to the original search query. You'll do the same thing for the other fifteen products. Once you get the ABSR of all sixteen products, add the numbers together and divide that number by sixteen. For example,

Total ABSR = 1,000,000 ÷ 16 = 62,500 average ABSR

You want an average ABSR of 100,000 or less. When a book sells at least one copy every other day, it'll place in the top 100,000 books. Books with an ABSR of around 10,000 sell about twelve to fifteen books a day. To have any real chance of success once your book launches, find an average rank between 10,000 to 100,000.

For a general idea of how well an ABSR performs, use the Kindle Best Seller Calculator available at DaleLinks.com/Calculator.

Can you select a keyword with an average ABSR below 10,000? Sure! Keep in mind the closer you get to #1, the more competitive and harder it'll be to sell your books. It's an all-out fistfight to get into the top 100 books, so be ready to do a lot of work to stand out from the pack.

Your list of keywords should significantly narrow down to roughly twelve to eighteen good selections. If it's under, don't sweat it. This exercise has you explore what is and isn't currently working in the market. As you note all the keywords, you're going to pay attention to a few other items:

- Categories
- Covers
- Book descriptions
- Number of reviews
- Length of the books
- Overall reader expectations

Since you're pretty new to writing and self-publishing, it's going to take some practice to size up the marketplace. Take your time! You need a basic understanding of what you plan to write before you ever write a single word.

CATEGORY ANALYSIS

In publishing, you'll hear two words used interchangeably—category and niche. The category explains the type of content readers come to expect in their books. When a book sells at least once, Amazon displays three categories for the title at the bottom of the **Product details**.

Also known as browse paths, the categories listed in **Product details** show where Amazon shelves a book. If you visit the category, you'll see similar books shelved together. Click the category to go to the **Amazon Best Sellers** list for the niche. On the left side of the page, you'll see the path it takes to get to the specific category. When you break it down piece by piece, you get the full browse path. For instance, if you click on the category **Sports Training (Kindle Store)**, you'll see it as a browse path:

Kindle store > Kindle eBooks > Sports & Outdoors > Training

Amazon allows you to select one to three categories for your books. You can list every print book and ebook in up to three categories, with rare exceptions to the rule. You will only ever see the three best-performing categories for a book in the **Product details**.

When you're on the **Amazon Best Sellers** list, browse the top twenty books. Look at their product page and their overall ABSR. Much like you did in narrowing down keywords, you're going to narrow down categories in the same way. If an average ABSR for a niche is between 10,000 and 100,000, you've found a great category worth pursuing. When you find an average ABSR below 10,000, then you know you'll have your work cut out for you after publishing. That's okay. Just remember, you will not have an overnight hit any time soon in this niche.

Once you've studied the categories and found at least three good ones, it's time to move on to the next most vital step—judging a book by its cover.

COVER ANALYSIS

Do not skip this step or take it lightly. You must study the popular and bestselling books based on their covers. Later, when you publish your book, you'll need examples of what is selling in your niche. Honor those elements and capture the niche's overall look and feel.

Again, you're still focusing on the top twenty bestselling books in a niche. Pay attention to common cover themes, fonts, colors, and layouts. Write down this info to help figure out what you'll do later once you publish.

Whether you're a fiction or nonfiction author, focus on the art and font selections. What assumptions can you draw based on the covers most popular in your niche?

While you're researching, copy each book's web address for later. You can use these examples to build out your future cover. When you study other covers in your niche, you'll grease your creative wheels and get something truly remarkable when you launch.

BOOK DESCRIPTIONS—THE MARKETING COPY

Once you have a good idea of what to expect in book covers, focus on the book descriptions. When visiting the top twenty books, select a book to view the product page and open the book description.

Though the book description seems like a synopsis, they serve more to entice the browsing customer into buying the book. Book descriptions are marketing copy—written content to advertise or sell a product. Copywriting is a much different craft than normal writing. The purpose of copywriting is to convert browsing customers into buyers. When marketing copy is on point, a book sells a lot. When the ad copy isn't any good, the book won't sell a single copy.

The bestselling book in a niche can provide clues on why it's selling well, including factors like the niche's popularity, cover, and marketing copy.

You should pay the closest attention to these elements in the marketing copy:

1. Length—how long is the book description?
2. Format—what is the overall format and layout of the copy? Are there single lines of text followed by a hard line break?

Or do you see blocks of paragraphs?
3. Keywords—what keywords do you see used in the marketing copy? Are there any relevant keywords you noticed in your prior research? How are those keywords used?
4. Miscellaneous—what other things do you notice about the book description?

Doing deeper research will help you unearth more ideas for developing and building out your content. Marketing copy will help you understand what other authors are writing and how you can fit into the niche.

OTHER RELEVANT FACTORS

The product reviews and length of the book are more factors to consider when browsing a bestselling book's product page. I mention them together since it all comes down to audience expectations. You can look at a bestselling book and know it sells dozens of books in a day. The issue lies in how the customers view the product. If an author publishes a book shorter than what customers like, then the reviews might be lower than usual. Conversely, if a book is longer than it should be, the buyers will also reflect that in the reviews.

First, pay attention to the length of the book. Then, scroll down and study the reviews. Skim through the four- and five-star reviews. You want a good idea of why readers enjoyed the content so much. Note anything worth covering for your own content. Go to the low reviews and look for the lengthier comments.

Figure out why a reviewer would give such low marks and capitalize on that misstep by avoiding it when writing your book.

Reviews reveal reader expectations. When an author nails it, they get four- and five-star reviews. Should the author fall short of reader expectations, you'll see that in the mediocre and lower reviews. Whenever you're in doubt about what readers want, visit a popular book in your niche and study the reviews. You'll learn a lot there.

COMPILE THE INFORMATION

Since you're still new to the business, you're probably wondering what you do with the information. This reminds me a lot of my high school Spanish class. For the first year, most of the content made little to no sense. Once I studied and practiced the language long enough, I comprehended it better.

You'll find writing and self-publishing to be the same. Don't worry about understanding it all at once. It takes time and practice.

Compile the information in a notebook or on your computer. You should have a list of keywords, categories, and examples of book covers and descriptions.

It's time for a challenge.

With the information you collected, draft a tentative title for your work. Do this with data and intuition. Go with your gut when selecting a title. Though it's not mandatory to include a keyword in your title, it may help in online discoverability.

For fiction authors, this may be easier said than done. If it's a stretch, then don't sweat it. Nonfiction authors have it much easier. Rather than loading up your title with as many keywords as possible, pick one or two good keywords, then organically weave them into the title or subtitle.

When in doubt, lead with an attention-grabbing title, then load up the subtitle with your relevant keyword. It appears more tasteful and a little less forced. You don't want your title to seem like it's trying too hard. Remember, you're titling your book for people, not an algorithm. All the best search engine optimization practices won't do you a lick of good if it's a turnoff to browsing customers.

We're only picking a tentative title now. We can decide on the final one later.

OUTLINING YOUR CONTENT

Nope, don't you dare skip this chapter! I see you rolling your eyes, and I assure you, it's not what you think. Writing your book can be a smoother process when you consider one missing element—outlining. When you outline a book, you simply sketch out a rough idea of how the book will read. Think of it like a detailed table of contents.

Back in the day, when I would go on a long road trip, I'd visit the local AAA travel office, and they'd whip together a TripTik. This road map guided me from point A to point B, with a few fun stops along the way. Nowadays, you have the luxury of online resources like Google Maps to do the same process.

Outlining your content works much in the same way. A few things are certain in writing your book:

7. You want to write a book.
8. You want to finish the book.
9. You want to publish the book.

You can mosey your way through your book and eventually get it done without an outline. But to complete your manuscript efficiently, arm yourself with an outline.

There are three types of writers:

1. Pantser—these are writers who simply write with nothing more than a rough idea. The term comes from writing by the seat of one's pants. Another term for this is "discovery writing."
2. Plotter—some writers strictly adhere to a structured format and rarely deviate from it. Outlines are their lifeblood. The term comes from having to plot out every detail.
3. Plantser—this is a healthy mix of improv and planning.

The plantser writer can be flexible while still staying on track to complete a manuscript. When you have a plan and allow for some deviation, the writing process will run smoother.

Plotters have a plan and stick to it. The issue with being a plotter is when something falls apart during the writing process. Does the plotter have enough wiggle room to allow for some improvisation? And will it affect the manuscript adversely? Some experienced plotters know what to do when a writing issue arises. Most newbie plotters will get hamstrung, throw out the manuscript, and start over.

Meanwhile, the pantser simply hopes to finish the manuscript sometime soon. The issue is you can miss market demands and reader expectations if you're writing a manuscript with no goal other than completing the book. Many aspiring authors believe pantsing is for them.

In the hit TV series *Family Guy*, the family dog, Brian Griffin, is forever writing his book. He considers himself a writer for the longest time, yet has no work to show for it. I've met many people like this fictional character. Their main issue is that they're too busy dreaming of what they can do, start writing with no direction, then quit when they lose their place or sense of purpose.

Try all three models for yourself. I feel the most helpful writing style is a mixture of both pantsing and plotting. Outline your work with the intention to stay on track and deviate when you see fit.

BRAIN DUMP

To make the outlining process easier, get it out of your head and onto paper. Since you studied the marketplace and know your niche relatively well by now, I'm sure you're bursting at the seams to get your ideas out right away. If not, don't sweat it. As you brain dump, you'll find it becomes like a snowball rolling downhill—the more you jot down, the easier the ideas flow.

Spend about a half hour to an hour writing out all the things you want to include in the book. No idea is unworthy, so write everything down. Even if you feel you're breaking off the beaten path, go with your flow of thought. Don't worry about the order or how you write it.

Just do it!

Once your brain-dump session is over, walk away. Don't write or even think about your outline. Create some distance between you and your topic. Absence makes the heart grow fonder. Later, when an idea hits you, add it to your notes.

Let your notes grow. Once you feel the well has run dry, get to work sifting and organizing. First, find winning ideas and concepts, then place a priority tag on them. After that, move on to the next part—outlining.

SECTION 1: WRITE

ORGANIZE, PRIORITIZE & QUESTION

Can you write your book based on a brain dump? Sure! I wouldn't recommend it since you can write yourself into a corner. After you sift through your content, prioritize your concepts.

Put your content in a logical order, like a table of contents. Put overarching themes as the main chapter headings. Then, any items relevant to an overarching theme should be placed under that main chapter heading. Break off any microconcepts under that.

Use relevant questions to stimulate creativity when you only have general themes and chapter headings. Have you ever seen how inquisitive children think? They always ask, "Why?"

Why, why, why?

The more questions you ask, the easier it is to supply the answers.

Ask the following questions:

1. Who?
2. Where?
3. What?
4. When?
5. Why?
6. How?

As you jot down these questions, you may find you need to organize the words logically. Go ahead! Circle back around and do it after completing the outline. Much like when you gather notes from the brainstorming session, step away after you're done to get some distance. Return to the outline later, read through it, and fill in the blanks as you see fit. Add more questions or refine your current crop of questions. Slip in some bullet points to make it easier for you to answer questions later. The deeper the outline, the easier the writing will be.

Don't go overboard and fence yourself in to be strictly a plotter. You need some flexibility. If creativity hits you mid-writing, you can work in content where you see fit. Once your outline seems like it's ready, get to work!

WRITING YOUR FIRST DRAFT

When writing your book, it's important to remember the following:

Your first draft will always be your worst draft.

I give you full permission to write the worst hammered garbage on this side of the Mississippi River. You're not writing a book that'll get immediately published. The first draft is merely a warning shot to the world. Much like a sculptor starts with a lump of clay, you'll start with yours, too. Just keep writing and staying consistent so you complete the manuscript right away. You'll sort everything else in the upcoming steps.

Write until you have a finished first draft. Since you have your outline set, simply start answering the questions you filled out for each chapter. At first, you'll start slow, but as you pick up momentum, you'll find the process progressively easier.

To be clear again, don't sweat perfection! You have permission to write complete and total drivel. While you're at it, shut down your inner editor. It's not welcome here. The more your inner editor intervenes, the harder it is to finish your first draft. Be okay with making mistakes and typos. Just keep pushing forward. Avoid using Backspace or Delete on your keyboard. If you're writing by hand, break off your eraser and throw it away. But you're not allowed to throw away any paper. If you mess up, keep writing.

HOW TO WRITE THE FIRST DRAFT

I'm the last person to tell you exactly how to structure your work or workflow properly. That's what's nice about having an editor. They'll sort all that out. For now, how do you write your first draft? What if you aren't very good at typing? Here are some options to consider:

1. Handwriting
2. Typing
3. Voice dictating
4. Transcribing

WRITING YOUR MANUSCRIPT

Handwriting might not be the most efficient way to do things, but go for it if it gets the job done. The biggest issue you'll run into is transcribing handwritten notes to digital. You may have to type them yourself or hire a typist to do it for you. This can be an added cost for you to consider if you hire out.

Time how long it takes for you to fill a single page or roughly three hundred words of content. Once you have a general idea of how long that takes, you'll know how much time you need to complete your first draft. Carve out time accordingly.

TYPING YOUR MANUSCRIPT

A majority of authors type their books. Whether you touch-type or chicken peck your way through it, typing can be the second most efficient way to get the job done. The biggest issue with typing comes down to how many words you can type per minute. Like writing your manuscript, it's a good idea to get a ballpark figure of how fast you are. Search for any online typing test to find out how fast you can type, then plan your schedule based on how long a full manuscript will take to complete. Later, you'll learn more about how much time you'll need and why.

VOICE DICTATING AND TRANSCRIBING YOUR MANUSCRIPT

More authors than ever are leaning into voice dictation and transcription to get the job done. Whether using dictation software or hiring a transcriptionist, dictation is the fastest way to complete your first draft. Voice dictation can work two ways: using software or recording your voice for transcribing later. Studies estimate that dictation software can be three times as fast as touch-typing.[i]

Though dictation software seems easy at first, it comes with some hang-ups. The problems include incorrect punctuation, misunderstood words, and inappropriate sentence structure. Again, a sound editing process and an editor will help clean up your manuscript.

When you dictate your manuscript, treat the process like an interview where you answer all the questions in your outline. As you finish each section, check it off and move along.

When using dictation software, you must be mindful of how it works before you bite into your project. After all, some software programs don't record your voice but translate your voice into text as you speak. Premium software like Dragon NaturallySpeaking will record your voice so you can review the transcript with the audio file.

My preferred method of dictation is to record and send the audio file to a transcriptionist. It costs more but is far less time-consuming. I'd much rather spend my time doing things other than struggling with wonky or unreliable dictation software. If you're going to record your voice, you can use your computer or mobile phone. Whatever comes at your disposal for no investment will work. I use my PC's built-in microphone and the free audio software Audacity. It's an intuitive program with tons of free online resources showing you how to use it.

Once you record the audio file, you can send it to a transcriptionist and simply wait for your first draft. I'll insert my preferred transcription services in the resources section of this book.

GETTING THE FIRST DRAFT DONE ASAP

Never play darts wearing a blindfold in a crowded bar. For one, you'll probably play a game you never intended to play. Also, you'll end up frustrating yourself or hitting the wrong target altogether. Apply this analogy to your writing goals.

If you don't see what you're doing, how can you even know the direction you're going, what you're doing, and what you want to accomplish? I heard it once said that vague goals bring vague results.

If you want to get anywhere in the business of writing and publishing, nail down what you're doing and how you'll do it. I'm not asking you to sacrifice your firstborn. I don't expect you to give up multiple hours per day to figure out your goals. It simply comes down to the whole SMART acronym:

1. Specific—be precise about what it is you'll accomplish.
2. Measurable—if it's not quantifiable, how will you ever know if you completed it?
3. Achievable—make your goals realistic according to your skill set and time.
4. Relevant—does it apply to the direction you're going in business and life?
5. Time-bound—have a deadline; otherwise, you'll forever be writing manuscripts no one will ever read.

Most authors come up short when planning goals because they don't have a deadline and measurable outcomes. There's a difference between saying:

"I want to be rich!"

And …

"I want to earn $100,000 per year within the next five years."

Now that you know four ways to produce a manuscript, how do you set your goals? After all, the plan needs to embody the SMART method.

Begin by measuring your efficiency. How fast are you able to produce your work? If you handwrite, how long does it take to write a full page with 300 words? If you type, evaluate your skills through any online typing test. Of course, if you're a talker, see how well you can

SECTION 1: WRITE

speak using dictation software or a voice recorder.

For the latter method, you'll see how much you write if you're using dictation software. If you record your voice, you may not know how many words you can generate until you transcribe the audio file.

Once you know how much you can produce in a given time, pick your end goal. How long will your book be? When researching your niche in the previous exercises, note the page length. A single page has about 250 to 300 words.[ii] If a book is 350 pages long, you can estimate it to have about 75,000 to 105,000 words.

Keep in mind these are rough numbers and will vary based on the formatting and layout of the published manuscript. Also, the page count varies based on the reader's expectations for a given niche. For instance, it doesn't make much sense to write a 120,000-word fitness book when a majority of the successful books in this niche are around 30,000 to 50,000. Conversely speaking, an epic fantasy novel might require a larger word count, exceeding 100,000 words as a minimum. These rough examples aren't an accurate reflection of those niches but more so a way to illustrate my point.

Not all books and reader expectations will be the same, so it's on you to research everything ahead of writing.

After you know how many pages and how many words per page, work your way backward from there. How much time will you need to devote? How many days will it take? Account for off days and holidays. It's unrealistic to expect you'll write every day of the week with no time off. Give yourself some wiggle room to get it done.

For instance, I know I can type about 2,000 to 3,000 words per day. The manuscript will most likely be about 30,000 to 40,000 words as a first draft. With the pace of my schedule, I know I have maybe three to four good writing days in me. This means it'll take me roughly twenty to thirty-two days to complete my manuscript. That'll take about five to ten weeks to complete.

Let's assume you have limited time. Use that time wisely and focus on a long-term goal to complete your manuscript. Also, analyze your day and see where you can sacrifice time to work on your first draft. It won't be easy, but it'll be worth it. If you find you're not gaining good ground and aren't mentally committing to short bursts of work, consider focusing on the word count. If you only have five minutes per day, use those five minutes wisely. Make it your goal to focus on the words written.

Whatever you do, never give up. Stay consistent with your efforts. Daily writing would be ideal in a perfect world, but we don't live in a perfect world. Do what you can with the time you have. Try not to take long breaks between intervals of writing. Otherwise, you'll lose your place, forget about what you were writing, and have to reread the manuscript before pushing forward.

Fiction author Martin McConnell shared in his book *Finish the Damn Book!* how daily writing will save you from having to rehash old work. Instead, the content will be fresh in your mind if you write daily or at least consistently. I couldn't agree with him more. Many abandoned manuscripts happen because of extended breaks between each writing session. Rather than rehashing or rereading the previous work, it almost always seems practical to throw away your manuscript and start again. I wouldn't recommend that, but sometimes, it might be the easiest option if you've had too many starts and stops.

SECTION 1: WRITE

One last note and something worth repeating—your first draft will always be your worst draft. Be okay with writing hammered garbage or content that is rough around the edges. You'll clean up any issues or discrepancies in the next step—editing.

SECTION 2: EDIT

After finishing your first draft, it's time for a celebration. You finally achieved what most aspiring authors don't, so treat yourself. Just don't take long, because much like writing the first draft, you want to attack the manuscript while the work is fresh in your mind.

Allow at least one rest day before working on your manuscript again. Absence makes the heart grow fonder and allows you time to marinate in your victory.

FIRST PASS EDITS—BEFORE THE EDITOR

Two camps exist on editing your first draft. On one side, we have authors who prefer sending the raw manuscript to their editors. No first-pass self-edits. No attention from the writer after the final keystroke. The editor gets the first draft in all its ugly glory. The other school of thought is to clean up the manuscript before torturing a human editor.

I'm sure you know by now that getting an excellent editor won't come free. If you find an experienced editor giving you free work, don't let them go! The chances of you finding an editor willing to work for free are slim to none.

SECTION 2: EDIT

Since you'll be plunking down your hard-earned dollars, it might be a good idea to mitigate any wasted movement for your editor. Why invest in an editor if all they're doing is correcting your typos and weird sentences?

Expect to go through three passes before sending your draft to your editor. It'll get you more familiar with your work and allow you to fix minor discrepancies with a few tools.

Start your first edits with simple grammar checkers. Since I write my manuscript in Microsoft Word, I use their **Editor** feature. This option finds misspelled words, wonky sentence structure, and other minor infractions. The first pass will not be about reading everything line by line. It's just a quick and simple cleanup. Move efficiently through the edits and make decisive actions. Don't sweat it too much if you can't figure out what you are saying. You may not even keep the offending line where you're stuck.

My next pass is very similar, but I'm dropping it into a different grammar checker this time. My go-to is the premium software ProWritingAid. Can you use the free version? Sure, but you limit some capabilities ProWritingAid has. Much like the first pass, I'm going through as quickly as possible while ironing out any minor indiscretions.

The next layer of editing requires my ears instead of my eyes. I use text-to-speech. Not all word processors have text-to-speech software, so research the options based on what you use. For Microsoft Word, you can use the **Read Aloud** feature (Alt + Ctrl + Space). Adjust the reading speed and voice type so you can sit back and listen to your book.

The biggest issue with self-editing is you'll miss most problems. Your brain has a bit of cognitive bias and glosses over issues without you even noticing. When using text-to-speech for editing, you'll hear blatant issues. It's a good idea just to listen and not read along. This separates you from the manuscript and allows you to be more discerning with the content.

When listening to your manuscript, take notes and be very present. You can't be on social media or answering emails while doing this task. It needs your undivided attention.

When you hear an issue, pause the software, fix the discrepancy, and place your cursor back at the front of the sentence or paragraph to listen back. Don't make the mistake of fixing an issue without listening to the sentence again. You need to hear how the sentence flows after fixing it. I used to make the mistake of fixing the problem and moving on, only to later discover I misspelled a word or made the sentence sound even worse.

The only things you need to worry about now include minor typos, misused words, redundant words, and sentence structure. Don't get too deep into your edits because we're going to let the professionals oversee all that. You don't want to remodel your house only to discover the foundation was built on quicksand. Much like the first few passes, you're going for quick and easy edits—nothing fancy.

What you're not doing in this last pass is rewriting. Again, you're creating a lot of work for yourself that may end up getting tossed out when your editor attacks the manuscript. Don't dwell long on this process since the first draft will undergo the most significant changes once your editor handles it. Be okay with some iffy passages or weird sentences. Your editor might help bring out the best approach later.

Once you complete these four quick passes, take a break! You've earned it. You're going to move on to the next, most vital step in the writing and publishing process—getting an editor.

HIRING AN EDITOR

Hiring an editor is like finding a good car mechanic or repair shop. It's going to take time, and you're going to kiss a few frogs before you find that one prince. Not all editors are equal, and every editor comes with their own skills, experience, and mindset. Finding a professional who gels with you and suits your needs can be rigorous and exhausting. Once you find the right one, you won't have to worry about the vetting process again.

Before finding the right editor, know the different types of editing and how it works for your manuscript. On most occasions, you'll find an excellent editor who specializes in all types of editing. Double-check before you hire so you don't miss getting the best services for your book.

Can you go with any sort of editor? Sure, but you have to remember the edits aren't merely for improving your book. It's about improving the reader's experience and building your credibility as an author. Don't take editing lightly, and never skimp on getting an editor for your manuscript.

TYPES OF EDITING

There are four stages of editing, and each of them will play an important role in the journey of your book before it launches. Consider editing in the following order:

1. Developmental and structural editing
2. Line editing
3. Copyediting
4. Proofreading

The purpose of developmental editing (also called content editing or substantive editing) is to look at the bigger picture.[iii] Remember how I had you clean up your manuscript and remove as many errors as possible? The reason we did that was to allow the developmental editing process to go smoothly. Why slow down your editor with silly mistakes and typos when they could be focusing on what you're trying to communicate in your book?

The job of an editor is not to "fix" issues in your manuscript. The editor's job is to shine a spotlight on what the issues are and help you find ways to address them. With the developmental edit, you'll get notes in your manuscript and sometimes also an editorial report. An editor who worked with me on my fitness books used to provide me with a one- to three-page report covering all the items that needed fixing. These notes not only helped me with the manuscript I was working on but also helped me to refine my approach to future books.

After developmental editing, a structural edit improves the structure of your manuscript. This is probably where I'm weakest in my own writing. I try to just go with the flow of my thoughts, but then my ADHD brain likes to go where it wants. Structural editing reels in the banter inside my head, dials down the dialogues, and places everything in a more logical order. Most structural editing should be easy if you followed the steps for outlining your manuscript. Should you have a paragraph or two out of place, it might be a simple case of moving or removing it. With structural editing, you're making the reading experience free-flowing and effortless. That way, it's not jarring or boring to the reader.

The next step is my least favorite—line editing. Thankfully, an editor will do the heavy lifting here. A line editor will analyze the text line-by-line for the 3 C's—clear, concise, and compelling.[iv] Line editing is one of the most arduous steps in the entire editing process because you have to see how a sentence reads both on its own and within the context of the paragraph or page.

After you've established context behind your words through line editing, you'll polish your manuscript for clarity through copyediting. This step focuses on grammar, syntax, and issues with style.

The final step and last line of defense in the editing process is proofreading. To be clear, there is a difference between editing and proofreading. Rather than having an entire chapter devoted to proofreading, I felt it just fit perfectly in this chapter.

Have you ever seen an automatic car wash? You load your car into the conveyor. It gets pulled through the machine, soaked with soap and water, and battered with giant cylindrical sponges. The final step before the car wash is over is waxing and drying. That's proofreading. Your manuscript went through the wringer and is now ready for one last pass to make sure it's all ready to go. Proofreading makes sure your manuscript is showroom-ready.

Though you can hire a proofreader for a fraction of the cost of an editor, I don't believe this is necessary. Proofreading is more of a "nice to have." If you're unable to afford one, consider reaching out to a few peers or readers interested in your niche.

All a proofreader needs to do is look for minor discrepancies. They don't focus on developmental, structural, or line editing work. Their sole purpose is to catch any typos, errors in punctuation, formatting issues, or anything that would distract a reader's eye from your message.

I prefer to lean on early readers for proofreading. You can reach out to anyone interested in reading an advance copy of your book. Even if you don't ask, they'll probably send you some notes anyway. Just take any feedback you get with a grain of salt. Not all opinions are facts, and you may not agree with all of them.

Some editors will include fact-checking or book doctoring. These two options can help when you don't want to do it yourself. If you're writing nonfiction, it's critical to cite your sources and double-check your facts. When in doubt, hire out. Get somebody else to do the fact-checking for you.

Speaking of cost, how much will it cost to hire an editor? Won't any one person do for all of your editing needs? Don't settle for less when it comes to your editor. Could you find someone willing to edit your book for free? Sure, but you won't get the same quality as you would from an experienced editor or a professional familiar with your niche.

Search and ask around about qualified editors. Look for an editor who is familiar with your niche—bonus points if they know your work already. Avoid anyone who you think may be biased. This means you should avoid asking a relative or loved one to edit your manuscript, because even if they are an experienced editor, you won't get the thorough and in-depth analysis you would from an editor you aren't close to or know intimately.

SECTION 2: EDIT

COSTS FOR EDITORS

I'm sure some of you have already skipped to this section in the hopes of getting an exact answer. Sadly, I'm going to have to let you down by just giving you general rules and guidelines. Depending on the type of editing, you'll pay varied amounts.

Editors typically charge based on one of the following factors:

- Word count
- By the page
- By the project
- By the hour

Usually, you'll find decent editors priced as low as $0.01 to $0.10 per word. A 100,000-word manuscript can cost from $1,000 to $10,000 for editing. That might seem like a lot of money, but oddly enough, it's actually at the low end of editors' rates. Remember, this is an investment well worth it in the long run.

Rates vary based on the type of editing. Proofreaders can run on the lower end at about $0.01 to $0.02 per word. In contrast, developmental editing might run closer to $0.10 to $0.49 per word.

When paying a per-page rate, you'll probably see fees ranging from $1.50 to $15.00 per page. Again, proofreaders will charge toward the lower end, while developmental editors will charge a higher premium.

Then again, some editors prefer to focus on a single project and offer a complete package. That won't be a short stroll in the park. When an editor signs on to a project, they'll typically work with you for weeks to months at a time. Most editors who function on a per-project basis typically charge a higher-than-normal rate. I've known some editors to charge for packages in the tens of thousands of dollars. Once you enter into an agreement with an editor willing to do a project, you'll practically be married to them for a while. Choose your editor wisely before settling with them.

Though I used to be completely against hourly editing work, I've since found a wonderful editor who I trust. She doesn't jack up her prices, and she turns around my manuscript within reasonable times. While her notes are firm, they are more than fair and help me tweak my writing style to better suit my readers.

WHERE TO FIND EDITORS

The best way to find an editor is through word of mouth. At first, it may seem nearly impossible to get a referral. Hang out in indie author communities, Facebook groups, or online forums where you might be able to get referrals from other authors. Don't be afraid to ask around. Most editors function as independent contractors and need work beyond one or two clients.

Though you may not know an author in your niche personally, it might still be a good idea to reach out to them and ask who they use for editing. Authors are more accessible than ever through social media or email. Reach out to someone in your niche, and see if you can get a recommendation and contact info.

The next resources you can look into are editing or freelance websites. Places like Reedsy, Upwork, Fiverr, and a host of other sites are available to you. Check out the Alliance of Independent Author's (ALLi) Watchdog Services list where they vet author services. Visit DaleLinks.com/Watchdog, type "editing" into the search bar, and get dozens of choices. ALLi even rates the sites based on the quality and history of service.

Once you find a good editor, don't let them go. Try to keep an open and consistent dialogue with them. Finding and keeping an editor is paramount to the success of your self-publishing business.

HOW TO SELECT THE RIGHT EDITOR

Many aspiring authors have squandered their money producing their manuscript. One of the major areas where this happens is in editing. Why? Because many authors sink a ton of money into an editor only to find out they aren't a good fit. You must try a few editors before before committing to just one.

Pick a sample of your manuscript you haven't edited or doctored, and send it to your potential candidates to get a sample of what they can do. Many editors will charge you for this sample, so be selective about how much you give them.

Your sample shouldn't be less than one page or longer than one chapter. Wait for all the samples to come back before reviewing the work. You're looking for the following:

1. Quality turnaround—was the editor able to complete the sample in a decent time?
2. Communication—did the editor give you detailed notes about your work?
3. Corrections—was the editor able to spot any minor issues such as typos and syntax?

Compare and contrast the three samples before deciding on who you'll choose. It might take a little back-and-forth dialogue with each editor before you settle on one.

How do you feel about the notes? Does your editor have your best interests at heart? Or is their commentary a bit too critical? I had a coaching client who said his editor would snidely comment on his work. She said if he didn't follow her edits, his work would never be successful. I personally wouldn't have minded the comment, but it felt like an insult to him. Thankfully, if you order a sample, you can avoid what he did—spending a lot of money on services that left him feeling demeaned and dismissed.

You must gel with your editor. After all, this relationship needs to be collaborative with the greater good in mind. If one person isn't on board, then the whole train could run off the tracks. Be careful about who you let in. Your editor needs to know your end goal and how they can help you turn your lump of coal into a diamond. Find the right editor, and you'll hit pay dirt in no time. Get the wrong editor, and you'll be forever mining coal.

When you finally publish your book, check your reviews. If your editing isn't as tight as it should be, you'll likely to hear about that from your readers in the comments. Discerning readers beat up scores of self-published books in the reviews section, all because the editing was subpar. To avoid that, find an editor who'll help you create a book to read and remember for ages to come.

AFTER THE EDITING

Once you get your first round of edits done, take your time and go through your editor's notes. Remember, your editor has your best interests in mind. Never take personally what an editor does. They only want to see your book succeed.

Where you might think writing the book is the hardest part, it's actually the editing. Now you have to go through all the editor's notes and address any markups on your manuscript. At first, you might see a manuscript riddled with red marks, but relax! It's perfectly natural to see that. Take a deep breath, and get to work.

If you don't understand why an editor made a correction, communicate with them. Never simply agree to a correction you don't understand and move on. An integral part of editing includes refining not just your manuscript, but also your overall writing style. For instance, I'm horrible about using passive voice in my writing. Whenever my editor busts me on passive sentence structure, I make a mental note to clean it up on my next first draft or in future corrections.

After I make adjustments, I go into my next round of passes. I like to repeat what I did before I sent the manuscript to my editor—Microsoft Word Editor, ProWritingAid, and text-to-speech. Once I complete those corrections, I'll send the manuscript back to my editor for a second pass. This pass shouldn't take nearly as long and will help refine any corrections I made from the first edit.

Once I get the manuscript back, I do it all over again. This time, I'll go a little slower using text-to-speech and pay close attention to how it all sounds.

The last step is to send your manuscript to a proofreader or a set of beta readers. You've already learned why a proofreader is important, so what's the deal with a beta reader? Beta readers will have a chance to read your manuscript before it's formatted and sent off for publishing. Rather than plunking down your hard-earned cash for a proofreader, you can always get readers who are most interested in your writing or your niche.

Instead of using beta readers, you could send out advance reader copies (ARC) and hope your readers will message you with any corrections, but that removes one layer of protection. Having an additional audience read your book before the ARCs acts as an insurance policy. I'd recommend this as a kind of safety net for your book before you pre-launch it to the public. With an ARC team, they get access to your book before it hits the market. In return, they'll leave a review of your book once it's live online. Having a rather large ARC team can present its own set of issues. You might get tons of notes and emails from your ARC readers with corrections you need to make.

By the time your ARC team gets your manuscript, you should have it formatted and ready to go. Sadly, if ARC readers find any issues or mistakes, you'll then have to go back, make the changes, and reformat your manuscript. Worst-case scenario, your ARC reader might even ding you for those mistakes in their reviews.

Beta readers will safeguard you from having to make corrections before the ARC team and subsequent book launch. Get about three to six beta readers. They need to have a keen eye for detail, enjoy your content, and be interested in your niche.

SECTION 3: FORMAT

I'd love to share the intricacies of formatting your manuscript, but trends and requirements change all the time. Any information I present here could be obsolete by the time you read this book. Also, you'll discover formatting a book isn't quite that easy and requires a separate publication just to learn what you should do.

I don't want to leave you empty-handed, so I'll give you a basic understanding of formatting and the steps you need to take based on the type of book you plan to publish. With three formats—ebooks, print books, and audiobooks—I'd have my work cut out for me, and you'd have a ton of studying to do. For now, let's stick with the need-to-know information.

FORMATTING TYPES

Print books, ebooks, and audiobooks all have unique formatting and have very little overlapping work. While you can produce a manuscript and format it easily for ebook and print, it becomes more problematic when producing an audiobook. Hang in there because I'm going to share later why all three have their place and why audiobooks are worth the extra effort.

EBOOK FORMATTING

For ebooks, you must convert your manuscript into two different formats:

1. Epub—most book distribution platforms use this file type.
2. PDF—this universal file type is great for almost any device. It can prove problematic on some platforms, though. I typically create a PDF file simply for advance reader copies. Beyond my pre-publishing strategy, I rarely go back to the PDF file unless it's for print copies. (More on that later).

The good news is you don't need a degree in computer science to format your manuscript into any of the aforementioned file types. A free and easy way to get a basic manuscript formatted is through an aggregate publishing platform like Draft2Digital (D2D). You don't have to publish on their platform to use their automated formatting software.

First, let's get some basic formatting things out of the way. I'm going to give you advice based on my experience with Microsoft Word. You should be able to use the same advice regardless of the software—Google Docs, Pages, and OpenOffice, among others.

1. Start with a completely blank manuscript.
2. Open your completed manuscript.
3. Press CTRL and the letter "A" to select all.
4. Press CTRL and the letter "C" to copy the text.
5. Go to the blank document and paste the text. For MS Word, you'll access the **Home** menu, select the **Paste** drop-down menu in the top left, and select the **Text Only** option. It's

the clipboard icon with the letter A in the bottom right. If you can't find this choice on your program, look for how you can paste unformatted text.
6. Now, highlight your complete manuscript again by pressing CTRL and the letter "A."
7. Justify the text so it fills the lines between each margin. Press CTRL and the letter "J."
8. Find each chapter title, highlight the text, and make it **Heading 1** under the **Home** menu. If you have any subchapters, use the **Heading 2**. Continue adding sub-subchapters under the other Headings of **3**, **4**, **5** or **6**, if applicable.

If you have any other bullet points or lists, format them accordingly. Avoid using any graphs or charts, since these are more labor-intensive and require the assistance of an experienced graphic design professional. If you want to go it alone, get access to my beginner's course where I show you some general formatting rules. (Visit DIYPubishing.biz/Free.)

Then, save your document as either a .doc or .docx file. Visit my referral link at DaleLinks.com/D2D to set up a free account at Draft2Digital. Go through the intuitive publishing process. Once you reach the next-to-last step, you can select from many templates for formatting your manuscript. Download both the .epub and .pdf file types.

Later we'll discuss where you'll need these formatted interiors and what to do with them. For now, hang onto them. In *Promotional Strategies for Books*, I discuss how these two file types are great for building your advance reader copy team. If you want details on how that works, grab a copy. For now, know that having these three file types will save you a lot of heartache in the long run.

PRINT BOOK FORMATTING

While formatting is relatively simple for ebooks, print books are twice as hard. You need to know many things before trying to format your print book. I like Draft2Digital for ebook formatting, but I can't fully endorse their print-ready files. I imagine in due time, D2D will come up with far better tools for print books. For now, I'm going to give you some tough advice.

You're going to need to hire out for this step. Although not ideal, this scenario will result in a better product and free up time for other areas of your self-publishing business. Again, if you're headstrong and cash-strapped, then grab access to my free course for beginners at DIYPublishing.biz/free. The interiors you create will be fairly rudimentary, but at least you can do it yourself and save a few bucks.

For print book formatting, you must know your book's size or trim and the paper type. When you researched your niche, you should've noticed popular trim sizes for print books. Go with what your niche most frequently publishes. From there, research what each publishing platform offers and if they have the quality you expect. I'll discuss a couple of options later.

No book about self-publishing will tell you precisely what you need to select for trim size or paper type. You'll find that most popular self-published books use the standard trim size of 6 inches by 9 inches (15.24 cm by 22.86 cm). It changes when you look at other categories like manuals and workbooks, which are usually published in sizes ranging from 8 inches by 10 inches to 8.5 inches by 1 inches (20.32 cm by 25.4 cm to 21.59 cm by 27.94 cm).

A general rule of thumb when it comes to paper type is that if you're publishing nonfiction books, use white paper. When publishing fiction, use cream paper. If you're publishing full-color books, then the paper defaults to white. There are exceptions to these rules. Study your niche to see what other popular and bestselling authors use for paper types. Visit your local library and browse the catalog for your niche.

Once you get your manuscript formatted, you must have the file saved as a PDF. Every major print-on-demand platform uses PDF files for book printing. Format any images you submit in 300 dpi (dots per inch) or greater so you get the best print run possible. Also, justify your text so that it fills the page from margin to margin. I can usually spot a self-published book when I see left-justified text, so for a better reading experience, be sure your book formatter justifies the text. You'll learn more about hiring a book formatter in the chapter about the cost of self-publishing.

AUDIOBOOK PRODUCTION

Audiobooks are trickier to publish than their ebook and print counterparts. Creating ebooks and print books is easy with word processing programs, but creating audiobooks requires expertise in recording and producing audio. While I applaud authors who record their own audiobooks, most should avoid doing so unless they have prior experience or professional help.

You must have your audio content saved as an MP3 file. The audio specifications become more problematic. Most audiobook distribution platforms offer a set list of requirements. You can find the following list on Audiobook Creation Exchange (ACX):

- Consistent overall sound and formatting
- Opening and closing credits
- All mono or all stereo files (never both)
- A retail audio sample between one and five minutes long
- Each chapter/section of your book should be its own file with the section header read aloud
- Per-track running time of 120 minutes or less
- Room tone recordings at the beginning and the end. It's the sound in the room with no extraneous noises.
- Measurement of between -23dB and -18dB RMS
- Peak values and noise floor no higher than -3dB and -60dB respectively
- Bitrate of 192kbps or higher with a constant bitrate at 44.1 kHz[v]

If you're anything like me, you probably don't know what half of those specs mean. That's why I leave it to the pros. Even when I recorded my first audiobooks in 2020, I relied on a professional studio and experienced sound engineer to manage all those details.

I'd rather be writing my next book or marketing my current crop of books instead of learning how to understand noise floors and decibels. If you're someone who is not comfortable narrating your own books, you'll learn about more options in the publishing chapter. The good news is you can hire many experienced narrators (also known as voice-over talent) to read your book. Unless you have experience recording and speaking for prolonged periods of time, narrating your books is best left to the pros.

Eventually, you can consider narrating your own audiobooks. Again, you'll learn about these finer details of publishing audiobooks in the next chapter.

BOOK COVER DESIGN: DIY OR HIRE OUT?

Readers can and will judge your book by its cover. You cannot expect to get any real traction in this business without an excellent cover. Most publishing platforms will have you believe the cover creator tools and templates they offer are sufficient. I've got bad news for you—they suck. There's no exception to this rule. If anyone uses a platform-integrated cover creator tool, they can expect few sales and no long-term success. I don't know of any successfully published book that has a cover that was made with a cover creator tool.

If you decide to use a cover creator tool, you need to be aware of a bigger issue. Though platforms like Kindle Direct Publishing (KDP) provide this option, it's mainly for beginner authors without big ambitions. Hundreds of thousands of authors publish through the KDP platform every day, but only a fraction of them use the cover creator tool. Though robust in templates and flexibility, the problem lies in the fact that the covers end up looking like one another.

To stand out from the pack, you must go beyond designing a book cover based on a template someone created in a stuffy cubicle at Amazon headquarters. You have two choices: either create your own book cover or hire out. I suggest that all new self-publishers outsource the cover creation process.

Your time is best spent on writing your next book or hyping your upcoming launch. Good cover design takes hours for most professional book cover designers. Now, imagine creating your cover with no experience. You essentially have to do brain surgery with nothing more than a few online tutorials and a willingness to learn. Skip the learning curve, and simply hire a pro. You'll thank me!

When funds are an issue, many authors consider using a cover creator tool or designing their own cover. Hey, I get it! My earlier books had lovely cover art that I designed. The book covers I created seemed great, and even my friends agreed. The harsh reality was those covers sucked. It wouldn't surprise me if customers wanted compensation for even looking at them.

It all comes down to time versus money. If you have more time than money, consider learning how to format yourself. Remember, though, that's time you could spend in other areas of your writing and publishing business. When you have more money than time, you should definitely hire out for the more complex tasks such as formatting and cover design. I know the feeling of not being able to afford a cover designer. When I couldn't swing the cost, I typically picked up a little extra work on the side or sold a few belongings to afford it. It's up to you and what works best for your lifestyle, time, and expenses.

The research you did earlier should've given you a good idea of winning cover design concepts. Grab a link to each cover you thought was good and use it for inspiration. Inject elements you'd like to see that best embody your writing. Note the font type, layout, imagery, and use of color. Share what you have with your cover designer.

Should you wish to do it yourself, then at least check out some of the best no-cost solutions for creating book covers. They are:

- GIMP—GNU Image Manipulation software is free graphic design software with a huge learning curve. Download a copy at GIMP.org. Also, you can find quite a few tutorials about GIMP on YouTube by Davies Media Design and Logos by Nick.
- Pixabay—This online image and video resource has creative commons licensing, meaning the images are free to use while no attribution is necessary. I highly recommend significantly altering images you use so you don't run into issues. Because these images can be used by anyone, the odds of an unedited image appearing on another cover design is very high.
- 1001 Fonts—This font website offers a ton of free and premium font licenses. Many self-publishers overlook font licensing, and unwittingly violate someone's intellectual property and copyright. Some fonts are available for commercial use. Other fonts require payment to use or aren't for public use. Search for the free fonts on 1001 Fonts. Once you find one you like, download it, install it, and use it. Keep in mind, not all fonts are usable for ebook or print interiors. Save any font files you have with the rights release information.

In early 2016, I had a decent handle on the free, open-source graphic design software called GIMP. The learning curve was steep, and I spent every day trying to navigate this beast of a program. I was eyeing up my recent launch of *An Ultimate Home Workout Plan Bundle* and the dropping sales. Though the dip in revenue wasn't terrible, it was enough to draw concern.

I had picked up the original cover through a cover designer on Fiverr for a whopping seven bucks. This cover had generated thousands in revenue by this point, so I didn't want the gravy train to stop. In my infinite wisdom, I thought changing the cover could bolster more sales. In theory, it makes sense to change a cover if sales are lacking or dead altogether.

For twelve hours I painstakingly toiled over GIMP to create a masterpiece. I nabbed some stock image licensing, tweaked the graphics more to my liking, and found just the right fonts to match the imagery. Before I published the cover, I thought I'd poll my friends and family. Everyone loved it! Why not pull the trigger and publish the update?

Within a day, KDP updated my book with the new, self-made cover. And sales came to a screeching halt. It was beyond brutal. Rather than pull the plug and go back to the original cover, I decided to tough it out for another month, thinking it needed time.

Nope. The buyers voted, and everyone agreed the cover was trash. I switched the cover back to the original design, and, lo and behold, the sales increased drastically. This just goes to show if it isn't broke, don't fix it.

When creating a cover design, you need to put your ego on a shelf and know that when book sales are low, it's usually for a variety of reasons. Improve the cover design, and sales should improve. When the cover design is bad, you won't even be able to sell a single copy.

I'm sure you're thinking:

> Dale, that's all well and good, but I can't afford a cover designer.

Remember that it cost me only $7 to get a decent cover design in my previous example. Can you get a good cover design for that cheap every time? It's debatable, but it's worth a shot when you don't have many alternatives. Rather than rushing your book onto the market, find ways to save for a quality cover design service. You'll learn more about the book cover design cost in a later chapter and find recommendations in the resources section of this book.

Assuming you don't have the money and can't afford to save it, you will probably have to do it yourself. Prepare for two things to happen:

1. Mediocre to low results in book sales.
2. More time spent learning about and working on cover design.

As mentioned before, online cover creator tools are a no-go. The best alternative for the cash-strapped author is going to be free software. GIMP is my preference, while others speak highly of online Photoshop-alternatives PhotoPea and Canva. When you first see these tools, you'll probably feel a bit overwhelmed and won't even know where to begin. The good news is you're only a Google or YouTube search away from your answers. When in doubt, search it out.

TYPES OF COVER DESIGN

All three publication types—ebooks, print books, and audiobooks—come with requirements and specs. You have some flexibility with ebooks and print books. With downloadable audiobooks, the requirements are strict, and you shouldn't try to deviate.

For all covers, you'll want to have picture quality around 300 dpi (dots per inch). The higher the dpi, the better the image quality. This higher resolution is perfect for print quality and looks fantastic on all devices—desktop, laptop, and mobile. When a customer searches for your book, they'll see a high-quality image. With ebook covers, you have a little more wiggle room and can adjust your image quality down to 72 dpi. Format in 300 dpi so you have a high resolution that prints crisp images.[vi]

For ebooks, you'll want your dimensions around 1.6:1 ratio. For example, your image will be about 1,600 pixels high by 1,000 pixels wide. I wouldn't recommend having your ebook cover image that small, though. All publishing platforms have a minimum requirement, so review the guidelines for each one to be sure. Ideally, format your ebook cover to be around 2,560 pixels by 1,600 pixels.

The other issue is file size. While you might have a stellar cover, you need to be mindful of the size of the file. When creating finer details with a higher dpi, you might run into large file sizes. Unless you're going above 300 dpi, you shouldn't have any issues. Again, review guidelines for each platform. In general, you can avoid many of the issues associated with large files by keeping your file sizes below 50 MB. That's a lot, and you shouldn't need so much.

Avoid using 3D images of a print book for your ebook cover design. Though it might seem attractive, it can be misleading. When a customer buys your book, it could confuse them when they only get an ebook and not a print book. Stick to a normal 2D ebook cover image, and focus on making it the best quality you can.

Print books are a bit more complex. Since the cover has to wrap around the book, you need artwork for the front cover, spine, and back cover. With all print books, the cover needs to account for an added measure called bleed.

Bleed is an extra amount of space or border around the printed text on a page. This extra space allows for slight deviations at the printer, so they get a good quality cut every time. When producing a print book cover, you must add 0.125 inches (3.2 mm) around the edge. Make sure your image spills into the bleed area while being mindful of any important visual elements that fall inside that bleed. The most important rule is to keep text away from the bleed area. You don't want important text to be cut off in the printing process. Be careful!

Figuring out the measurements for your front and back cover is rather simple. What is the trim size of your book? A 6-inch by 9-inch book will have a front and back cover that each measure 6 inches by 9 inches (15.24 x 22.86 cm). To determine the spine size, you'll need to know the page count of your book.

No, you don't use the page count of your ebook. You'll need the exact page count of your fully formatted print book interior. KDP has a great formula for calculating your spine size:

(Paper Thickness) x (Page Count) = Spine Width

[(Trim Height) + (2 x 0.125" (bleed)] = Spine Height

[(Spine Width) - (0.0625" (spine area margins)] = Max Size of Any Text on Spine[vii]

What if you don't want to do math today? I feel you on that one, so that's why I use KDP's book cover template generator. Now, I'm not going back on my word about their book cover creator tool. I'm recommending using the simple calculator KDP offers that configures the basic layout based on your paper type, trim size, and page count.

A complete print book cover will look like the book opened up and laid out flat. From left to right, you'll see the back cover, spine, and front cover surrounded by the bleed. Once it's all set, save your file to PDF since all publishing platforms accept this file type. Make it easy on yourself and create both your interior and cover as PDF files.

For audiobook covers, you must honor the same elements you did for the ebook and print cover. The tricky part is you need it in a square format. For most audiobook publishing platforms, format your cover to 2,400 pixels by 2,400 pixels. I recommend going with 3,000 pixels by 3,000 pixels so you can use an Amazon-alternative platform called Findaway Voices (more on them later).

All audiobook publishing platforms will take the cover at 3,000 pixels by 3,000 pixels as long as you remember these few rules when creating your audiobook cover:

- Save your image as either a jpg or png file.

- Your image is no smaller than 2,400 pixels x 2,400 pixels.
- Your image should be 72 dpi or greater.
- Format your image a true square, not a rectangular image with borders.
- Don't stretch your ebook cover image.

The last rule is a biggie. In my first years in the business, I naively believed stretching the ebook cover to create an audiobook would suffice. My audiobook sales suffered because the covers always looked like amateur hour. When I switched my audiobook covers to the proper ratio and developed the covers to the square specs, my audiobook sales exploded.

When hiring a cover designer, I highly recommend using the same designer for all iterations—ebook, print, and audiobook. Express your needs, and share the specs above. Ask for both a 3,000-pixel by 3,000-pixel image as well as 2,400-pixel by 2,400-pixel image. If they charge extra for getting both, ask for the larger size since it's easy to resize the image yourself.

Do not phone this in. You'll get far more sales if you simply put in the little extra effort and invest a little more upfront.

SECTION 4: PUBLISH

Before you publish on any one platform, you need to identify your ultimate goal. A few questions to ask yourself include:

- What do you want to accomplish with this book?
- What will be different about your life later because of this book?
- Are you publishing for profit or pleasure?
- Do you want more readers or more money?

The latter question is one you need to answer outright. The answer will be different later, but right now as a newbie author, what do you want to achieve more than anything? Would you like more people to read your book? Or is it more important for you to make money from your writing?

MORE READERS VERSUS MORE PROFITS

Some experienced authors will have you believe you can have both. While this advice is sound for experienced authors, it's not practical for beginners.

In this book, you're getting need-to-know information. Once you get your self-publishing business running, you'll at least have the fundamentals of the industry. You can tweak your direction and diversify your business later, but for now, stick with the basics.

MORE PROFITS

Go with the platform that is dominating the vast majority of online publication profits—Amazon. It's the path of least resistance and only requires a little time and sometimes no money if you're resourceful enough. Over 70% of online publication profits come through Amazon,[viii] so why not get a piece of that pie?

As a new author, publishing to Amazon Kindle Direct Publishing (KDP) is a simple decision. You get 35% to 70% of book sales made through over a dozen different regions and countries, not to mention your title will have a spot on a platform that sees millions of visitors a day. Learning how to publish on the platform is super easy. Between Amazon KDP's Help page, online articles, and YouTube videos, most anyone can learn how to do it with some time and patience. So why not go with KDP alone?

The biggest reason you shouldn't rely solely on KDP for publishing your books over the long term is simple. You don't want to place all your eggs in one basket. Yes, a vast majority of self-publishers have zero issues with publishing on the platform. While it's safe to say you might be one of those thousands with no problems, there are still a select few who accidentally run afoul of the Amazon Guidelines.

If Amazon boots you off the platform, there's very little you can do beyond appealing your case or moving on. Many authors who appeal are unsuccessful in doing so. Amazon KDP has a ton of overwhelming guidelines that are chock full of legalese. It's no wonder self-publishers violate the rules. While you might try your best to abide by the rules, Amazon can still kick you off or change the rules with no advance notice.

I shared in *Promotional Strategies for Books* how a prolific romance author I knew lost all his business one day. He didn't have a website, an email list, or assets on any other platforms. This man was pulling in over six figures per month, and it all ended when Amazon kicked him off the platform. He didn't know what he did or why they discarded him. What can you do with this information?

I'm not trying to scare you away from publishing through KDP. It rewards more people than it penalizes. I just want you to see the long-term vision of your business. Part of your business strategy should include publishing beyond Amazon and bringing in readers from more than one platform.

MORE READERS

You don't want to rely solely on Amazon with your first book. Let's explore publishing to various platforms—also known as publishing wide. While Amazon carries most online publication profits, they don't have a monopoly on all profits or all readers. In fact, quite a few readers avoid Amazon and would rather go to places like:

- Apple Books
- Barnes & Noble
- Kobo
- Google Play Books
- Any platform that sells via Ingram Content Group distribution

By publishing to more platforms, you'll diversify your business and reach more readers. The biggest issue you'll run into is receiving lower royalties from Amazon. That's okay, because most of the time the sacrifice will be worthwhile. We're going to explore further what you stand to lose or gain by publishing wide while using Amazon KDP for distribution.

Some platforms will treat you well and give you a fair payout. On other platforms, you'll find a considerably lower royalty structure than what KDP offers. For instance, if you want library distribution, use platforms like:

- Overdrive
- Bibliotheca
- Hoopla

Sometimes, you can charge more for your work when library distributors publish your work. Other times, you will get a fraction of your sales price based on a per-checkout model or subscription-based pool system. That's the sacrifice you have to make if you want to have your books in the library systems. Do you want your book in libraries? That's completely up to you and something you need to consider when publishing wide.

KNOW YOUR RIGHTS—PUBLISHING EXCLUSIVE TO WIDE & BACK

Publishing each version of your book comes with a distinct set of rights. You can publish an ebook exclusively on Amazon using KDP Select without affecting the distribution rights of the print book or audiobook.

The same goes with publishing your audiobook exclusively through Audiobook Creation Exchange (ACX). Though the ACX exclusivity agreement covers the audiobook version of your manuscript, it does not pertain to the ebook or print book.

Here's the fun part of the business: should you not wish to publish any one iteration of your book, you can choose to sell the distribution rights for that iteration only. Let's say you don't want to go through the hassle of publishing your audiobook. You can sell the audiobook distribution rights to a publishing company and keep the rights to your ebook and print book distribution.

Would I recommend doing this? No. This is merely to illustrate the point that distribution rights are different for whatever iteration you're publishing.

When publishing wide, you have the option to choose all platforms or stick to one platform. Some authors choose the KDP Select Program for better royalties, ranking, and promotional benefits; however, this limits distribution of the ebook to the Amazon platform. KDP Select does not cover the audiobook or print book. You can still publish those wherever you like.

If you want to publish your ebook wide, then do not opt into the KDP Select Program. However, remember that if you later want to go from publishing wide to exclusive with KDP Select, you must fully delist your ebook title on all platforms outside of KDP. Conversely, if you want to publish wide after being in KDP Select, then you must opt your ebook out of the KDP agreement and, most times, wait out the rest of your contract period. You'll get a deeper understanding of what to do and how it works in the chapter about Kindle Direct Publishing.

SELECTING THE RIGHT PLATFORMS

For ease of use and simplicity's sake, you're going to need access to one to four options for publishing. Rather than make this process any more difficult than it has to be, you'll want to limit the options. Set up your free account for each of these platforms:

4. Kindle Direct Publishing (KDP)—kdp.amazon.com
5. Audiobook Creation Exchange (ACX)—acx.com
6. IngramSpark—ingramspark.com
7. Findaway Voices—findawayvoices.com

The first two options are best for first-time publishers. If you decide to forego the latter two, that's okay, but consider exploring those avenues eventually.

Setting up a publishing account on any of these platforms is fairly intuitive. Should you get lost, reach out to Support on the respective platform for help. While it's simple to set up a publishing account, setting up the payment and tax information can be tough. Authors living outside the U.S. have more hoops to jump through. I'd love to give everyone universal advice for filling out banking and tax info, but regional tax laws vary, and I'd likely lead you astray. To be safe, reach out to a good business attorney or certified public accountant if you need advice.

You must have your payment and tax info before you can publish. Though it's a pain to do, remember, you only have to do it once per platform. Once it's set up, you won't ever have to sweat doing it again.

EBOOKS, PRINT BOOKS & AUDIOBOOKS

The most successful authors are those who diversify their business. Can you publish only ebooks? Sure, but what about the readers who prefer physical books? Consider the readers who only want to listen to audiobooks. To reach a wider reader base, you need to publish in all mediums—ebooks, print, and audiobooks.

I've heard many would-be gurus tout how publishing audiobooks or print books is a waste of time and money. Well, they're doing it wrong if they're publishing only audiobooks and print books, because they're losing money and time. Readers love all types of content and don't gravitate to one specific medium based on the niche. The "gurus" merely say this for one of two reasons:

a) They want you to give them more money for their courses or coaching.
b) They're ignorant.

Kudos to the millionaire "gurus" who've built their business solely on ebooks. Imagine how much more they could have earned if they'd only taken the extra steps to honor all readers, regardless of the type.

As an example, you might start running ads on Amazon. A browsing customer might see the ad and click on it for more details. Maybe the ad was for an ebook, but the customer doesn't enjoy reading ebooks.

What will the customer do if given no other choice? They will leave. Can you blame them?

Let's say you have an author who diversifies their content and runs the same ad, thus giving the customer options. What if they dislike ebooks, but love print books? Well, now they have a choice. Even better still, imagine if they love audiobooks—bingo! They've got the option.

Diversifying your publishing portfolio can seem overwhelming for most beginners. In due time and with practice, you'll find it gets easier. If you lack the financial resources, I'd recommend chopping away at the options in the order they appear here:

1. ebooks
2. print books
3. audiobooks

Publishing ebooks can be very simple with a little practice. With print books, you're dealing with a more precise formatting method and exterior content. Audiobooks take more time to produce, especially when considering narration and production fees.

If you must forego one avenue, make a promise to yourself to come back to it when finances allow. In an ideal world, you won't rush your publication to market. Instead, focus on building out all three assets and then publishing them simultaneously.

PUBLISHING EBOOKS

The best platform for publishing ebooks is Kindle Direct Publishing. Since you already know Amazon pulls in the lion's share of the online profits, it's also good for you to know the regions where your earnings will come from. They are:

- United States
- United Kingdom—including Guernsey, Isle of Man, Ireland, Gibraltar, and Jersey

- Germany—including Austria, Liechtenstein, Luxembourg, and Switzerland
- France—including Monaco, Belgium, Switzerland, and Luxembourg
- Spain—including Andorra
- Italy—including San Marino, Vatican City, and Switzerland
- Japan
- Netherlands
- Brazil
- Mexico
- Canada
- India
- Australia—including New Zealand[ix]

With a baker's dozen of regional distribution, you can see why KDP is a simple decision for publishing ebooks. Every region comes with a different royalty structure within which you must account for currency exchange rates. While your title might list for $4.99 in the U.S., it might list for £3.78 in the U.K. You can adjust your price for each region should you want to have a rounded amount per sale. For example:

- $4.99
- £3.99
- €3.99

The tricky part of publishing ebooks through KDP revolves around what you should upload. The interior file types you'll need for publishing through KDP include:

- .doc or .docx
- .pdf
- .epub

The latter two options work best. If you want your ebook to have a specific layout, then you'll want to come with a fully formatted manuscript as an .epub. Authors who upload .doc or .docx to KDP will run into problems with KDP's automated formatting.

Authors who don't mind the layout of their book deviating slightly from their original manuscript can stick with .doc or .docx file formats. During my first few years of publishing, I used only .doc files. Yep, I relied solely on OpenOffice and then later Microsoft Word to format my manuscript. I wouldn't recommend using .doc or .docx if you want to have a more robust interior.

The biggest issue will come if you're using PDF. Though KDP accepts the file type, it'll make a complete mess of the interior. Instead, try to revert your PDF back to a .doc/.docx or convert to .epub.

Just heads up, though! Amazon loves ebooks with what's called reflowable content. Unlike a fixed layout, reflowable layouts allow the reader to change the font type and size while viewing your ebook however they want. With fixed layouts, the reader can only see your book one way. They can zoom in and out on the ebook, but it's a rather rigid reading experience.

Use fixed layout books if you must. Stick to reflowable layouts if you can.

Getting the interiors just right can be easy or a bit more labor intensive depending on your discretionary time and budget. My preference more and more is to hire out. Leave the formatting to the professionals so you can focus your time on higher-yielding results. Instead of spending time on formatting, you can promote your upcoming release on social media or in interviews online.

It all comes down to time versus money. If you have more time than you do money, then you're going to have to learn how to do it yourself. Conversely, if money isn't an issue, then hire out! Let's look at each option.

First, I could write and publish an entire book about proper formatting, but the biggest issue would be keeping it evergreen; I would have to update it every few years as technology renders my advice obsolete. If you want an in-depth look at formatting your manuscript, get access to *The DIY Publishing Course for Beginners* (DIYPublishing.biz/Free). I will show you exactly how to format your ebook and print book interiors.

For now, you can use these essentials for basic formatting:

1. Body—any content within your manuscript should stick to **Normal** formatting. Stick with a size 12 font, and don't deviate too far from traditional fonts like Times New Roman and Arial.
2. Heading—any chapter titles should be **Heading 1** while subchapters should fall in line with **Heading 2**, then **Heading 3,** and so on.
3. Images—if you must use images, keep the sizes below five inches wide and six inches high (12.7 cm by 15.24 cm). You will lose any layout options for the image, such as right, justified, or centered alignment. The KDP auto-formatting

removes image layout options and typically defaults to left-aligned.
4. Tables—avoid these at all costs. They get messy across all devices. If you must use a table, use the same measurements as images.
5. Lists—basic lists with numbers or bullet points can work. Once you go into deeper lists with subsets, it gets messy and will often publish incorrectly.

Beyond that, you're ready. With more complex interiors, I highly recommend hiring out. It's better to have someone do it for you, learn how they did it, and then experiment with future projects.

THE EBOOK PUBLISHING PROCESS

Now that you have a formatted manuscript, let's walk through the publishing process. Remember, some of these steps may or may not change in the coming years on KDP. The fundamentals should remain, so read through the process.

STEP 1: KINDLE EBOOK DETAILS

First, under **Create a New Title**, click the **Kindle eBook** option to start the process. The first step is the most important—entering your book's metadata. The metadata includes:

- Title
- Subtitle
- Series name
- Author name
- Description

- Publishing rights
- Keywords
- Category selection
- Age and grade range

You should already have a clear idea of the name of your book, so insert the title and subtitle. If this book is part of a series, circle back around and adjust it later. You will not have the same flexibility with your print book, so if this book is the first in a series, do some deep thinking now.

For your description, write out a suitable book blurb before moving on. Next, you'll want to format the description so it's eye-catching and will command a browsing customer's attention. KDP has a decent selection of formatting options like bolding, italicizing, underlining, and more. Take your time exploring the options to optimize your listing.

For Publishing Rights, select "I own the copyright and I hold the necessary publishing rights." The second option for publishing public domain books is worth considering if you lack original content to publish.

KDP states this about public domain work:

Our program allows the selling of content that is in the public domain; however, we may ask you to provide proof that the content you submitted is in the public domain. We may refuse public domain content that's already available through our program or other retail sites. If a free version of a public domain title is available in our store, we will only publish a differentiated version.[x]

I'm not a fan of publishing public domain work, but don't let that stop you from researching if it's right for you. My Content Manager, Ava Fails, wrote an excellent piece about it on my website (DaleLinks.com/PublicDomain).

After that, you have to disclose if you're publishing adult content. Amazon places this safeguard to block adult content from impressionable young minds. It will limit your discoverability, but it won't entirely hinder you either.

Next, you can select a reading age. For most titles, you shouldn't fuss with the ages or grade range. If you're a children's book author, young adult author, or erotica author, you probably should adjust the age range. Be selective about what you choose. When in doubt, go back to Amazon and study your niche. You'll typically see the reading age range of a title on the product page.

Now, select your primary marketplace—the Amazon platform you wish to establish as the homebase for your book. You must select this option in order to do the next step—category selection.

Amazon offers thousands of category variations. The deeper you go into a category string, the more precise you will be in identifying your readership. Select from one to three categories under which your book will be displayed. Think of it like putting your book on the right digital bookshelf. Don't overthink it. Choose what makes the most logical sense.

Your next step is going to be filling in the seven keyword slots. Do you remember all the keywords you researched in the earlier chapter? Now, we're going to put them to good use. Use your seven best and most relevant keywords in the seven slots. While some would-be experts will tell you to fill them to the brim with every word under the sun, I'm going to discourage you from doing that. Since it's your first book, you don't need to sweat more advanced keyword strategies. Remember, you can always come back later and update your keywords. That's the beauty of self-publishing—you can fix things in real time.

For a granular approach to keyword research and implementation, check out my five-time award-winning book, Amazon Keywords for Books. You'll get the precise steps for using the right keywords to increase discoverability.

The last option is for scheduling a pre-order. It allows you to display your ebook's product page before its actual release date, giving customers the opportunity to reserve a digital copy of your book. Amazon will gather all the sales and dump them into your dashboard on release day. It's actually a fun way to launch a book, especially if you have a solid marketing plan to drive sales during the pre-order phase.

If you don't want to set up pre-orders, you can instead opt to publish your ebook immediately. KDP will review your file after you finish the upload process, and the book will go live right away.

Click **Save and Continue** to progress to the next step.

STEP 2: KINDLE EBOOK CONTENT

Now you'll upload your manuscript and book cover and enter two more items for metadata. You'll want your manuscript and cover fully done when reaching this step. If you don't have them completed, you can always back out or hit **Save as Draft** at the bottom of the screen.

Starting at the top, you must make a big decision regarding Digital Rights Management (DRM). The purpose of this tool is to mitigate issues with pirating by limiting a consumer's ability to share the ebook. Though it's intended to hurt bad actors, it usually ends up saddling your readers with the burden of limited use. For instance, you can only read a DRM-enabled book on so many devices. If a reader has quite a few devices they use for e-reading, then they must pick or limit those devices because of DRM.

Pirates know precisely how to work their way around this safeguard. Heck, the public knows how to do it. Just search on Google or YouTube, and you'll see how easy it is.

I usually opt out of DRM. Once you hit publish on your ebook, you cannot change this setting. Choose wisely.

Your next step is to upload your manuscript. Again, you can use .doc/.docx or .epub file formats. You'll see KDP offers to accept KPF, but that's for their platform-exclusive word processor called Kindle Create. The big issue with using Kindle Create is that KPF only works for KDP. You can't use it anywhere else, so I recommend avoiding it.

Next comes the book cover. Do you see the **Cover Creator** option? You do? Good, now ignore it. You should have a book cover you made or had designed by a pro. Upload it under the **Upload a cover you already have** option.

Give KDP a few minutes to process your files. Don't keep trying to re-upload while it's processing. Much like pressing an elevator button repeatedly, it won't make the process go faster. Just upload once and KDP will show when your files have successfully uploaded.

The next step requires you disclose the use of generative AI (artificial intelligence). If any part of your book—text or images—was generated by AI, you must tell KDP how much you used it and to what extent. KDP draws a distinction between AI-generated and AI-assisted. With AI-generated, you're letting artificial intelligence create work for you. For AI-assisted, you're using artificial intelligence to help with grammar checking, outlining, or writing prompts.

You don't have to disclose the use of AI assistance, only AI generation. AI-generated content would include content written by ChatGPT or images created by Midjourney. AI-assisted would refer to tools like ProWritingAid or other spelling/grammar tools.

If you're unclear about how you should mark this box, contact Support through the **Contact Us** link in the bottom of your dashboard.

Scroll down and click the **Launch Previewer** option. Again, give it a minute to process the images.

Then scroll through your content and proof the complete manuscript. Look at it through different orientations and device types through the selection menu in the top right. Once you're satisfied, simply click **Book Details** in the top left corner to return to the main menu.

If you don't like the way it looks, you can always edit your manuscript, re-upload it, and then check it out again. Remember that if you have a reflowable layout, then what you'll see in the previewer is a rough idea. Your ebook's layout will change based on the device—mobile apps, Kindle e-readers, and more. Don't get too hung up on how it looks. Focus on making sure it's readable and professional.

The last part of this step is obtaining your Kindle ebook ISBN (International Book Standard Number). The ISBN is how the books are identified internationally. Though not required for publishing your ebook through KDP, an ISBN is great for publishing wide and getting listed as the sole owner of the imprint. The imprint is the trade name you want associated with your ISBN and book. When customers find your book, they'll see your company or brand name in the Product Details.

To get an ISBN, you can search your region-specific ISBN distribution site. For the U.S., Bowker has a monopoly on buying ISBNs. In the U.K., it's Nielsen. The more ISBNs you buy in bulk, the lower the cost. You pay anywhere from $1.50 to $125 for an ISBN, based on buying volume. In some countries like Canada, ISBNs are completely free. Research options in your region. If you have the option to get free ISBNs, I highly recommend that you do it.

Keep in mind you can only use an ISBN once for each product type. The ISBN used for your ebook will not work for your print or audiobook. Conversely, the ISBN associated with your print or audiobook won't work for your ebook.

Getting an ISBN involves a deeper dive, and I cannot begin to cover the intricacies of every ISBN agency. Visit your local ISBN agency and ask for help when you need it. Once you have an ISBN, enter the relevant details in the **ISBN** and **Publisher** spots.

Though you don't need to use an ISBN for your ebook, you can use a little workaround to include your name as the publisher. Leave the ISBN slot empty and then put your company name in the **Publisher** slot. When your book goes live on Amazon, you'll see your company name listed in the product details rather than the default tag of *Independently Published*.

Click **Save and Continue** to move onto step 3.

STEP 3: KINDLE EBOOK PRICING

The last part only has a few more steps to complete the publishing process. The first option is the most important on all the pricing set up—choosing KDP Select.

I briefly alluded to KDP Select in the previous chapters, but now it's time to address what it is and how it functions. KDP Select is a 90-day agreement that showcases enrolled ebooks on Kindle lending programs like Kindle Unlimited and Prime Reading. When a reader subscribes to Kindle Unlimited for a monthly fee, they're allowed to read up to ten ebooks at a time. These ten ebooks must be a part of the Kindle Unlimited program. Authors get paid based on the number of pages of their book that are read in a given month.

All subscription fees go into a monthly pool called the KDP Select Global Fund. KDP divvies up the global fund to all participating authors based on the total number of pages read in a month. At the time of this writing, each page read earns you less than half a cent. You won't get rich on a single customer checking out your book, but you can benefit from using the full system.

While you might make less money per book with the KDP Select Program, you get extra benefits that help you stand out from non-program authors. A few of the perks include:

1. Books borrowed through Kindle Unlimited influence the bestseller ranking
2. Five-Day Free Book Promotion
3. Seven-Day Kindle Countdown Deals (U.S. & U.K. only)
4. Increased royalty percentage in all global regions

Once your book sells, you'll see an Amazon Bestseller Rank (ABSR) in your product details. The ABSR system shows what products perform the best for a category. When you make more sales, your book will rank closer to the number one spot. Fewer sales puts your rank at a higher number. Every sale and lending program checkout influences the ABSR of a book.

If your book is in the KDP Select program, when a reader borrows it and reads even a single page, your ABSR improves. This is the unfair advantage KDP Select authors have. Obviously, the better your ABSR is, the more likely Amazon will be to share your book with other interested readers. An author in the KDP Select Program can become an Amazon Bestselling Author without ever selling a single copy. Let that sink in for a moment.

The Amazon Bestseller Ranking system has this flaw. You can publish a bestselling book without ever having sold one copy. That's why KDP Select offers an unfair advantage.

While this sounds enticing, it doesn't work as well as you think. First, you're going to need hundreds of thousands of page reads before you ever see the same financial return of a single purchase. Next, you must have tons of borrows before seeing any real, lasting results or an ABSR worth bragging about. Last, not all niches are a good fit for Kindle Unlimited. Fiction readers use the Kindle Unlimited program the most. It's been my experience that nonfiction readers aren't quite as voracious.

Rather than trying to publish wide on your first book, consider publishing your ebook in KDP Select to get all your ducks in a row. The ninety days will give you long enough to determine if KDP Select is a good fit. During that time, you can always investigate other ebook publishing platforms.

Books enrolled in KDP Select also get two free promotional tools: the Five-Day Free Kindle Book Promotion and the Seven-Day Kindle Countdown Deal. You benefit from having your book showcased in special categories for free books or Kindle Countdown Deals.

Leverage the Five-Day Free Kindle Book Promotion option to gather more reviews and get word out about your book. At one time, this strategy built relevancy with Amazon's algorithm, but it's outdated now. Use this promotional method to give your readers a taste of what's coming or of who you are as an author while generating more honest reviews on the platform.

Use the Seven-Day Kindle Countdown Deal to bolster sales while keeping your royalties at 70% (more about royalties later). On the U.S. and U.K. Amazon sites, your book will have a pre-determined sale price as a limited-time offer. Just below the "buy" button will be a countdown clock. This timer creates a sense of urgency for anyone visiting the page and should coax them to buy your book. Be careful about how you share your Kindle Countdown Deal since it's only available in the U.S. and U.K.

Another catch is that you can only use one promotion type during your 90-day exclusivity period. While you can break up how many days you use at a time, you cannot split the days between the two promotional strategies.

If you're not getting any downloads or sales, don't expect KDP to promote your book to their customers. That's the thing—Amazon loves selling products. If you're proving your worth on the platform, they will reward you with traffic. If you aren't doing a single thing, then Amazon won't give you squat.

Market and promote any time you use the Five-Day Free Book Promotion or the Seven-Day Kindle Countdown Deal. While some avenues return significant results, no one method is suitable for everyone. For now, just share your KDP promotion so you aren't relying on Amazon to do the work for you.

Grab a copy of my four-time award-winning book, <u>Promotional Strategies for Books</u>, to learn more about how to market and promote your book on Amazon.

The last perk you get for enrolling is additional royalties in select regions. Normally, in Brazil, Japan, India, and Mexico, you only get a 35% royalty no matter what you price your ebook. With KDP Select enrollment, you get the full 70% when pricing between $2.99 and $9.99.

READ THIS BEFORE ENROLLING IN KDP SELECT

If you enroll in KDP Select, you can't publish your ebook on any other platforms during the ninety-day agreement. Anyone wishing to publish wide should avoid opting into the KDP Select program. Once you check the box to enroll in the program, your contract will auto-renew unless you go back into your settings and deselect enrollment.

Even if you deselect the option after enrollment, that doesn't mean your title is out of the program. Once your ebook is in the program, it's stuck there for the entire ninety days. To remove your title from the KDP Select Program before it ends, reach out to KDP Support via the "Contact Us" feature on your dashboard. You can request to remove your title from KDP Select while forfeiting any earnings from your enrollment.

I don't recommend removing your title from KDP Select mid-enrollment. It looks suspicious to Amazon KDP reps and could bring you unwanted attention. It's best to deselect enrollment and wait out the ninety days. Once your title is out of the KDP Select program, you'll see **Enroll in KDP Select** as an option when hovering over the ellipsis button at the right of your title. If you select the **Promote and Advertise** button, you'll see KDP Select as an option at the top.

Next in your publishing setup, you will need to select distribution rights for territories. If you wrote your content, then you own the distribution rights. Select **All territories**. If you do not own the full distribution rights and someone else has ownership in a specific region, then select **Individual territories**. Deselect any region where you don't have permission to distribute. Again, if you're new to writing and publishing, chances are pretty likely you'll select **All territories** for distribution.

Now comes everyone's favorite part of the publishing process—**Royalty and Pricing**. When you researched your niche, you should've seen a general price point. In the event you didn't, go back and review the bestselling books in your niche. You'll want to add all the prices together of the top 20 books, then divide that number by 20 to get your answer. That is the average cost for books in your niche.

Before finalizing your book's price, note the differences in the royalty structure. KDP rewards authors who price their book within their preferred pricing range of $2.99 to $9.99. You will receive fair compensation of 70% royalty for each book sold, which is better than what traditional publishing companies give authors. Any books priced outside of that range fall into the 35% royalty range. Amazon knows its customers better than anyone. They want you to price your ebooks competitively. If you don't, then they'll penalize you with a lower royalty.

Should you want to price your ebook above $9.99, then go with $19.99 or greater. Here's how the math works:

Your ebook price = $9.99 x 70% = $7

Your ebook price = $19.99 x 35% = $7

It sucks eggs if you have a high-value premium ebook because your content will have the same reward as a lower bargain, cheaper-priced ebook. For pricing above $9.99, consider:

- Raising your price considerably
- Fulfilling orders through direct sales (i.e., your website, Gumroad, or Payhip), but remember that this option isn't available for KDP Select-enrolled books.

Based on the region you live in, you can change your **Primary Marketplace** to reflect your location. Once you have the royalty structure selected, enter your ebook price in the **List Price** box. I recommend keeping your price point just below the dollar. Let's say you want your book at $5, then shoot for $4.99. The same would go with the U.K. Price your ebook at £4.99 instead of £5. Some psychological triggers entice more buyers to invest below the dollar than on the dollar or any random number.[xi]

With that theory in mind, select the drop-down for **Other Marketplaces** and adjust all regions accordingly. Ignore the figure, including VAT. Instead, focus on the pricing in the box. For each region, you'll see the royalty for your title on the far right.

Should your title fall into the 35% royalty, you won't have to worry about delivery fees. For any titles falling into the 70% range, you need to deduct a delivery fee. The customer takes on this burden, but you still have to account for this in your bottom line.

KDP states the delivery costs are equal to the megabytes of your ebook. The larger the file you have, the more delivery fees you incur. It roughly comes out to about fifteen cents per megabyte and varies per region. The minimum fee you'll get is one cent. You'll want to read the fine print for delivery costs for a better idea per region on the KDP Help Page (DaleLinks.com/KDPDeliveryFees).

Next, you'll decide if you want your book loaned to other readers. Should a customer buy your ebook, this option allows them to share it with someone. The good news is they can only share the ebook with one person at a time for up to two weeks. While one person has the ebook, no one else can access it, even the buyer. I enjoy having this option because it allows readers to share my work so I can gain another reader.

Will you sacrifice some earnings at first? Sure, but if you focus on your long game, you'll know this non-buying reader might become a fan and invest in your future books. Sometimes, they might buy your book if it was fantastic.

Last, review KDP's Terms & Conditions. Though I've done my best to tell you what to be mindful of, the Terms & Conditions will help clarify some more gray areas. Admittedly, I've read it a few times, and it's really dry and chock full of legalese. If you are still unclear or concerned about any of the terms, consult a lawyer. I highly recommend Helen Sedwick, author of the *Self-Publisher's Legal Handbook*. She's an experienced indie author and attorney.

Now, take a deep breath and click the **Publish Your Kindle Ebook**. Once you hit that, the KDP team will get to work on vetting your book. The approval process can take from twelve to seventy-two hours. Sit back and relax. Allow KDP to do their job. Once your book is live across all regions, KDP will email you. If you don't see the email within three days, contact KDP through your dashboard using the **Contact Us** link.

Once you upload and publish the ebook, KDP will recommend publishing a paperback version of your ebook. I highly recommend using this option to transition easily from one product iteration to the other while maintaining some metadata. It's much less work than starting from scratch. Should you want to come back to do the print book later, you can always select the paperback option below your ebook listing. That way, you'll still have all the metadata ready to go for publishing.

THE PRINT BOOK PUBLISHING PROCESS

If you have a manuscript formatted for print, you can easily walk through the publishing process on KDP. Remember, some steps may or may not change in the coming years on KDP. The fundamentals will remain, so read through the process.

Since you read this book in order, all you have to do is continue the publishing process from the ebook. All the metadata should carry over, so there will be less for you to fill out. These instructions will follow a similar protocol, but I'll shed light on areas that are different in print publishing.

Before jumping into things, you need to know one huge point that could make or break your decision to publish print books on KDP. Amazon only offers paperback books with sixteen trim sizes, two types of paper, and two print colors. You can publish paperback books in the following sizes:

1. 5" x 8" (12.7 x 20.32 cm)
2. 5.06" x 7.81" (12.85 x 19.84 cm)
3. 5.25" x 8" (13.34 x 20.32 cm)
4. 5.5" x 8.5" (13.97 x 21.59 cm)
5. 6" x 9" (15.24 x 22.86 cm)
6. 6.14" x 9.21" (15.6 x 23.39 cm)
7. 6.69" x 9.61" (16.99 x 24.41 cm)
8. 7" x 10" x (17.78 x 25.4 cm)
9. 7.44" x 9.69" (18.9 x 24.61 cm)
10. 7.5" x 9.25" (19.05 x 23.5 cm)
11. 8" x 10" (20.32 x 25.4 cm)
12. 8.25" x 6" (20.96 x 15.24 cm)
13. 8.25" x 8.25" (20.96 x 20.96 cm)
14. 8.5" x 8.5" (21.59 x 21.59 cm)
15. 8.5" x 11" (21.59 x 27.94 cm)
16. 8.27" x 11.69" (21 x 29.7 cm)[xii]

You must have at least twenty-four pages to publish a print book. Based on the type of ink and paper you select, the maximum page count ranges from 550 to 828 pages. Be sure to read more on the KDP Help Page (DaleLinks.com/KDPHelp).

KDP offers hardcover books in five trim sizes with a more limited distribution. While your paperback will be available in twelve Amazon marketplaces with Expanded Distribution, hardcover books only reach eight of those regions. Unlike paperback, hardcover books must have a minimum of 75 pages and no more than 550 pages. In time, KDP may offer more trim sizes, distribution options, and page counts, so hang in there if an option you wanted is currently unavailable.

Setting up hardcover books is the same process as paperback books, as long as you're aware of some of the limitations imposed by Amazon specifically for hardcovers.

When publishing print books on KDP, black and white books are considerably cheaper to produce over the full-color premium options. The term "black and white books" refers specifically to the printed interior content—not the cover. If you're looking for vibrant interiors with full color, you must either charge more for your book or lose more money per sale.

Amazon KDP offers some standard color interior options for authors who want to have full color interiors. While KDP's premium full-color option uses thicker stock paper, the standard option uses thinner paper. This means if you have too much ink on the page (for premium color saturation), the book will warp. When the customer buys the book, it may arrive looking like it's been sitting in water. If your book is image-heavy, then the standard option might not work for you. Just know that when you sacrifice the premium option for a standard option, you'll limit the quality as well.

WEIGHING IN: KDP PRINT VERSUS INGRAMSPARK

You might assume I'm all-in with KDP, but that's far from the truth. I feel KDP is the easiest and most viable option for newbies. A select few indie authors want to hit more markets beyond Amazon, and I can't say I blame them. After all, you don't get brick-and-mortar (aka physical store) distribution through Amazon. That's why you also need to know about IngramSpark.

In 2013, Ingram Book Group launched IngramSpark to connect indie authors to a larger reading audience. Ingram has the largest and widest reach of all print-on-demand distribution platforms. In fact, Ingram has so wide a reach that even KDP uses them for their Expanded Distribution.

Do you want to make a little extra revenue with a few added steps? Would you like to have more print book options such as trim sizes, paper type, and print book quality than what KDP offers? Then IngramSpark might be the way for you to go. Do you want hardcover books or hardcover books with dust jackets? Then IngramSpark has you covered. While I won't share a play-by-play strategy for uploading your content there, I can assure you the process is fairly intuitive.

*When using KDP and IngramSpark, do **not** select the Expanded Distribution option on KDP since IngramSpark provides the same service. Meanwhile, you'll earn more money per sale through IngramSpark compared to Expanded Distribution on KDP.*

Please pay close attention here. The publishing process is "free" on IngramSpark. You can upload a book and publish it for no upfront cost, but IngramSpark will take a 1% distribution fee from each sale. They also charge a $25 fee should you need to update your manuscript sixty days after publishing. At that point, you are already out a few more bucks than you would have been with KDP. Do a little research ahead since Ingram occasionally offers coupon codes that reduce or waive the update fee.

One of my preferred ways of waiving the IngramSpark update fees is through a membership with the Alliance of Independent Authors (ALLi). Members of ALLi get on free update per month. Annual membership to ALLi costs around $119 per year. Should you update five times on Ingram within one year, your annual ALLi membership will pay for itself. For more details about ALLi, visit DaleLinks.com/ALLi or visit the resources page.

Something else to consider is that you may need your own ISBN to publish through IngramSpark. They currently provide free ISBN's for U.S. account holders, but haven't indicated if this option will expand to other countries.

WHAT IS AN ISBN?

ISBN stands for international standard book number. The ISBN is how all book retailers and distributors identify your product. When publishing to KDP, you can either take KDP's free ISBN or bring your own.

When you use a free ISBN, you can only use it on the platform where you received it. I liken it to cooking in my kitchen. You're welcome to use my kitchen, including access to my cookware and utensils, to make a meal. When you leave, you can't take my cookware with you since I own it. You can still enjoy your food however you like, just don't take my pots, pans, and other items used for your meal.

On the other hand, if you come to my kitchen and prepare a meal with your own cookware, then you can and should take your stuff with you. That's exactly how it works when using a purchased ISBN.

Using the free ISBN lists the distributor as the publisher of the content—not you or your company. When using ISBNs you own, you are the listed publisher, not Amazon or IngramSpark. You can use the ISBN you purchased anywhere and everywhere for your print book.

Once an ISBN is in use, you can do little to change the metadata. If you want to alter the trim size, print type, or anything else, you must publish a second edition. It's better not to change your print book details and content after assigning an ISBN unless absolutely necessary.

To buy your ISBNs, visit ISBN-International.org/Agencies for the region-appropriate site.

ACCEPTABLE DOCUMENT TYPES FOR PRINT BOOK PUBLISHING

Almost every print-on-demand book distribution platform accepts PDF for both the interior and cover. You'll find rare exceptions to the rule, and often the outcome isn't the best when using other document types. A PDF locks the content of your book so what you see is what you get.

The biggest issue with formatting print book interiors is that it can be a pain for newbies! If you don't have experience with Adobe InDesign or Microsoft Word, designing an interior can be difficult. You must account for the margins and the bleed line. This is all too much for a newbie to handle.

Instead of guessing or grinding your way through it, hire a professional. Similar to hiring an editor, rely on other authors and their recommendations. Referrals are the best way to find fully vetted and experienced professionals. Besides, you can easily ask other authors to see their work and know if the investment is worth it.

Even though I know how to format print interiors, I don't do it myself. Why? Because my time is better spent on writing my next book or promoting my backlog. I hire out so I can focus on other aspects of my business.

Look into freelance platforms like Fiverr or my preferred formatting service, Miblart. Before you plunk down money, review the freelancer's portfolio so you can make an informed purchase. Order a sample to see if they'll be a suitable match, and if you think they can capture your vision for the interior.

Be sure your print book cover file is a PDF that is at or above 300 dpi. Anything else will not work for publishing your print title.

Once you have your print interior and cover done, you're ready to move onto the next step. It never hurts to get another set of eyes to look over your formatted manuscript and cover. All you're looking for is constructive criticism and any typos that need to be fixed before launching. You might think your cover design is flawless, but you can and will miss something at some point. Rather than allowing buyers to discover your mistakes, have somebody else find them before sending it to print.

STEP #1: PAPERBACK DETAILS

When you're setting up your paperback, the title, subtitle, series name, author name, description, and keywords will automatically carry over from the ebook you published. Double-check the information, and make sure it's correct. Unlike ebooks, once you publish your print book, you're stuck with what you have. You'll learn more in the next step.

One way in which the paperback setup will differ from your ebook is in the selection of keywords. The relevancy of keywords varies by product type. While the keywords you have for your ebook will work for most searches, it may not be as relevant for your print book. Once your book is live on the marketplace, it's a good idea to circle back and change your print book keywords. This requires deeper exploration and is something you should review only after finishing this book.

Check out Amazon Keywords for Books, where I talk about how to do product-specific keyword research.

After you change your paperback keywords, you will need to select your categories again. KDP doesn't carry over the categories you assigned for your ebook to the print book. Take a few minutes to browse the options and select one to three categories. Rather than using the browse paths from the ebooks, you'll use the categories specifically for print books.

Next, KDP will ask if your book contains adult content. They're not trying to entrap you with this question. Adult content is completely okay to publish through KDP (with some exceptions). Selecting this option will narrow your audience to adults only. Answer honestly if your book has language, situations, or images inappropriate for anyone under 18 years old. That's it. No tricks.

Then, hit **Save and Continue** to progress to the next step.

STEP #2: PAPERBACK CONTENT

The next step begins with filling out the ISBN. As mentioned before, you can choose to publish your book with the free-assigned ISBN or bring your own. I advise most newbies to stick with the free-assigned ISBN. It's less risky, and you can always come back later to publish a second edition with your own ISBN. If you do decide to publish a second edition, remember to delist the first edition in order to avoid market confusion and drive sales to the second edition.

Then you'll need to choose the publication date. Unlike ebooks, you cannot set your paperback for pre-orders, but you can schedule it for a specific release date. The book's product page won't appear to the public, but setting it for a future release date will allow you to order copies of your print book ahead of launch. Schedule the release at least four weeks ahead if you want to order and receive books in time for your official launch date. It isn't mandatory to order author copies or proof copies when scheduling your book for release.

If you want to set up preorders for your print books, consider IngramSpark. Don't sweat it if you can't set up a preorder. I don't know a single author whose booklaunch failed because they didn't set up a preorder for their book. It's nice to have, but it's not a necessity.

Next, select the appropriate print option:

1. Black & white interior with cream paper
2. Black & white interior with white paper
3. Standard color interior with white paper
4. Premium color interior with white paper

Then, select your trim size (as mentioned previously), the bleed settings, and the cover finish. Cover finish options come down to taste. Do you want to have a matte cover which appears flat and has a smooth surface? Or do you like the glossy, shiny surface with some reflective qualities to it? When in doubt, visit the library or a bookstore to see which cover finish is popular within your sub-genre or niche.

Next, upload your formatted interior and your cover. This will take some time for KDP to process. Click the **Save as Draft** button at the bottom, then come back to this step after KDP has finished processing the files.

You'll recognize the **AI-Generated Content** disclosure box from uploading the ebook. Answer the question honestly, and if you get stuck, contact Support.

Once the file is ready, check it in the **Print Previewer**. Be mindful of any notes or issues KDP identifies in the box to the left of your book preview. If any issues arise, you'll have to resolve them before you move on. Should you have questions, reach out to KDP Support, or contact your book design pro to troubleshoot.

Click **Save and Continue** to progress to the next step.

STEP #3: PAPERBACK RIGHTS & PRICING

As you've learned, publishing a print book requires more time, attention, and skills than publishing an ebook. While you do have the option of simply sticking with Kindle Direct Publishing for printing paperback books, you may miss out on off-platform opportunities.

Start by acknowledging rights for the various territories. Much like the ebook, if you wrote the work and it's 100% original, worldwide rights will be yours. In the event that you're publishing a public domain book, check the copyright for other regions. In that case, select individual territories and deselect the regions where you don't have distribution rights.

Moving onto **Pricing & Royalty**, you'll decide the best price point by averaging the prices of the top twenty books in your niche. Or if you have another price in mind, run with it.

You'll notice KDP offers two unique royalty rates. The first royalty rate is what you earn for selling your book on the Amazon platform—60%. Unfortunately, this does not mean you will get $0.60 out of every $1.00. This means that KDP will pay you 60% of the retail price minus the print fees. The extra fees come from printing the book and the number of pages. When it's all said and done, you'll be paid approximately 35% to 50% of your book's retail cost.

The cost of your print book needs to meet a minimum based on the print fees. Most titles have a minimum list price of $3.00. You cannot charge more than $250.00 for any one title. You'll see what your pricing range is under the **List Price** column.

Enter your preferred pricing, and allow KDP to calculate the royalty. To the right, you'll see the royalty rate, the printing costs, and the royalty amount. The last number reflects what you'll make for every sale.

Similar to ebooks, you'll want to set your **Primary Marketplace** in the drop-down menu. If your market is primarily in the U.S., then leave it at the default of Amazon.com.

Just below **Primary Marketplace**, you'll see an option for **Expanded**

Distribution. As mentioned previously, Ingram Book Group fulfills Expanded Distribution sales. This option only distributes to the U.S. and U.K. while other services like IngramSpark tap into all of Ingram Book Group's reach. By using KDP's Expanded Distribution, you only get a fraction of Ingram's total reach, so I discourage authors from using this option.

If you do choose **Expanded Distribution**, you'll earn a 40% royalty minus the print fees. You'll see you're getting over half of the royalty rate you would through the Amazon marketplace. Sure, you get distribution to thousands of retailers and libraries, but you also sacrifice a fair chunk of your royalties by selling through KDP. If you don't want to fuss with multiple publishing accounts with different companies, this option is for you.

Next, set the price in each of the regions. Unlike the ebook pricing model, the print pricing model per region is a little goofy. Where value-added tax (VAT) applies, you'll notice an additional figure to the right of your pricing box. Adjust the pricing box so the figure with VAT included comes out to just below the dollar. For example, if you price your print book at €13.26, the adjusted pricing with VAT might be around €13.99.

For the regions unaffected by VAT, price the book below the dollar. Again, that plays an important psychological factor in influencing customers to buy your product. Adjust your pricing however you wish, but be mindful of the adjusted rates, including VAT.

Once you set pricing, you have two options—you can either order a proof or you can publish. Since you're new to this business, I recommend always ordering a proof before clicking the **Publish** button. Reviewing a proof copy will allow you to make sure your title is 100% ready to hit the market. You don't want the formatting to be off or for there to be any major mistakes in your book.

Select **Request printed proofs of this book,** and Amazon will create a shopping checkout process for you. KDP will email when it's ready to order after your request, and you can go through the Amazon marketplace to checkout.

Fair warning! All proof copies come with a watermark band across the cover saying, "Not for Resale." If you wish to get proofs without the watermark, you must publish your book first, and then select **Order Author Copies** in the same line where you requested the proof. You won't see this option until you publish your title. You can buy pre-publication proofs or post-publication author copies at wholesale prices.

Buy author copies and keep some stock on-hand for trade shows or giveaways. I order about ten to twenty author copies of every book I publish. The wholesale cost of your book should run right around $3, depending on the number of pages and ink type.

Once you're ready to pull the trigger, click the **Publish Your Paperback Book** button. KDP will ask you to confirm, and once you do, the book will go through the approval process. You will get an email notification that your book is live on Amazon around one to three days later.

*Bonus tip: To access your ebook or print book in the various Amazon Marketplaces, go to your title in the dashboard. Hover your cursor over the **View on Amazon** link just below the pricing. A drop-down menu will populate with links to the various regions. Select the region you wish to visit, and you'll go directly there. Use the link for sharing your content.*

THE AUDIOBOOK PUBLISHING PROCESS

Though most indie authors publish ebooks and print books, few take advantage of publishing an audiobook. It's not a surprise considering the amount of work involved and the deeper investment. To diversify and future-proof your business, I recommend publishing downloadable audiobooks.

Ebooks still drive the most unit sales overall. However, ebooks don't generate as much profit per sale as print books do. When KDP started in 2008, many people believed that ebook profits would overtake print profits. But there is still a strong market for paperbacks which makes ebooks easier to sell at volume despite the lower profit per sale.

Meanwhile, downloadable audiobooks came out and started building relevance with readers. In many cases, such as with shorter nonfiction or novellas, the audiobook retail price can be less expensive than paperback. Audiobooks are private, convenient, and offer a reader more versatility in both the time and ways they can consume your book. Most audiobook apps have adjustable speeds, so listeners can enjoy their audiobook as quickly or as slowly as they want.

While many ebooks are inexpensive, they still require attention and energy to read. Audiobook listeners can set and forget. Just download the audiobook, press play, and enjoy the content that would otherwise need your undivided attention. Audiobooks are also great for people who want to multitask. Whether driving to work, exercising, or doing routine tasks, audiobooks serve as the ultimate companion in everyday life.

It's no surprise that downloadable audiobooks are on the rise. If you don't have audiobook publishing in your portfolio now, you'll regret it later. Where ebooks were in 2008 is where audiobooks are today. Get on it. You'll thank me.

Where do you go and what should you do to publish an audiobook? Will it require a ton of money, or can you simply publish it for free? Much like digital and print books, you want to go with the path of least resistance and to the place where the most listeners congregate—Amazon. To get to Amazon, we can use two to three viable options for audiobook distribution. As part of that distribution, you'll find qualified audiobook professionals to bring your manuscript to life. Let's look at these three avenues and what you can expect from each when producing an audiobook.

AUDIOBOOK CREATION EXCHANGE

Audiobook Creation Exchange (ACX) is a publishing platform launched by audiobook distributor Audible. This Amazon-owned company has distribution to Amazon, Audible, and, weirdly enough, Amazon's competitor Apple.

Distribution isn't ACX's only forte. The platform also functions as a marketplace for audiobook narrators and rights holders. Experienced and aspiring narrators alike can audition for audiobooks they're interested in. Rights holders are authors or self-publishers who want to have their audiobook narrated or produced and distributed.

In most cases, I'm totally okay recommending you do it yourself in self-publishing, but not when it comes to audiobooks. You must rely on a trained professional to produce your work. Unlike ebooks and print books, you can't get away with improperly formatted content. Audiobooks must adhere to strict audio specifications, or you will not get distribution. There's no exception to this rule.

If you intend to record your audiobook with your iPhone, you might as well forget about it. Subpar recordings won't cut it, and distributors will block your publication from distribution until you get it right.

Instead of doing it yourself, consider hiring a professional or finding a recording studio experienced in audiobook production. The best way to get it done? Hire a narrator.

There are three ways to hire a narrator on ACX:

1. Pay for production
2. Royalty Share
3. Royalty Share Plus

I recommend **pay for production** since you keep all publishing rights for your audiobook. Pay for production—also known as per finished hour (PFH)—is when you hire a narrator to complete your project based on the total length of your finished audiobook. ACX estimates an hour of read content is about 9,300 words.[xiii]

For example, if your book is 93,000 words, then your audiobook will be roughly ten hours of total listening content. ACX's estimate is not exact because narrators read at different speeds, and the content may influence the pace of the narration.

An experienced narrator runs about $250 PFH or more. Though you may find narrators willing to charge less, few will be as experienced or have the quality you need for your audiobook. Be selective with who you choose, and don't cut corners by hiring a bargain-basement narrator.

SECTION 4: PUBLISH

The narrator has to:

1. Read through your work
2. Prepare notes
3. Research pronunciation
4. Record the content
5. Edit the content
6. Mix and master the content
7. Upload the content
8. Make revisions when necessary

Though your finished audiobook might be only ten hours long, it may take four to six times longer than that to produce. Not to mention the software and studio space the narrator will need to meet the minimum quality specifications of each plaform. This means if you're paying a narrator $250 PFH and they produce a ten-hour audiobook, they'll get paid $2,500. Assuming it took them forty to sixty hours to produce, they'll get paid a modest $41.66 to $62.50 per hour. Based on their skill set and experience, it's really not that great.

Now imagine if you paid the narrator $50 PFH, and it took them forty to sixty hours to produce a ten-hour audiobook. You'd pay $500 total, while they'd earn roughly $8.33 to $12.50 per hour. Yes, they're sometimes paid at or below minimum wage. Yikes! If you're paying your narrator any less than $50, reconsider even publishing audiobooks.

I produced all my audiobooks for the *Amazon Self-Publisher Series* at a local recording studio. It cost me about $300 to produce a two-hour book. Though I'd like to think I'm good enough to record my book in two hours, it took closer to three and a half hours and another three hours to edit and master. Imagine if someone had paid me $50 PFH for the audiobook. I'd have lost money on the deal!

When selecting and negotiating with narrators, remember to calculate their expenses for time, experience, equipment, and quality. You never want to insult voice-over talent who's worth far more than you're pitching. Later, you'll learn how to find a narrator who fits your budget. Until then, let's address an option for anyone lacking the funds—the royalty share.

Also known as the 50/50 royalty split, this option allows a rights holder to find a narrator willing to do the work for half of all profits. This agreement locks both the rights holder and narrator into a seven-year contract that keeps the audiobook exclusive to the ACX platform.

With the royalty share agreement, you (the rights holder) don't have to spend any money to produce the audiobook. Instead, the narrator shoulders all the burden and risk to work on your audiobook. Should the audiobook take off and sell copies like gangbusters, the narrator should make more than their worth over the seven-year contract. Conversely, if the audiobook performs poorly, the narrator is the only one out on the deal. You didn't invest any money, so you only share half your earnings with the narrator—no matter how low those earnings may be.

I'm not the biggest fan of the 50/50 royalty split because of how long the contract is and the convoluted process of breaking the agreement. If your audiobook performs better than expected and you want out of the contract, you can't break it without the narrator's permission. Since the narrator owns 50% of the distribution rights for seven years, they will expect to be compensated for their time and share. Most narrators will offer an early termination buy-out option to break the contract, but they will inflate their buy-out price to make up for any losses caused by terminating the contract early.

You might think they would just ask for their finished price per hour as a fair rate of compensation. But if your audiobook is selling well, they stand to lose money by ending the seven-year agreement. They want their piece of the pie, and that's what they signed up for when they took your project on with no money paid up front.

As an example, I once had an audiobook pull in quite a few sales per month over the course of its first two years. I reached out to the narrator to terminate the agreement. I expected to pay his normal PFH, possibly a little over, to be released from the contract. Instead, he offered an astronomical figure. I knew I'd lose more money by opting out early instead of staying in. It turned out to be a great deal for him, but the royalty split in that case was a poor deal for me.

The deal works both ways, though. If a narrator wishes to end the royalty share agreement, reach out to ACX Support and explain the situation. ACX will delist your title. You can then republish the title as a DIY project and collect your full royalties. Sadly, you will lose any reviews on the product as you are starting anew with this quasi-second edition.

From my experience, the royalty split is perfect for anyone who is cash-strapped and has no other option. If you must use the 50/50 royalty split, then do it for your first book. Use the earnings from the first book to fund your next audiobook production. Then, pay outright for production instead of using the royalty share option.

Sadly, quite a few experienced narrators aren't willing to take the risk on royalty splits. That's okay, because ACX also offers a hybrid of the royalty split and pay-for-production model called Royalty Share Plus.

Any rights holders who want premium narrators can use Royalty Share Plus. The narrator will bring down the PFH pricing in exchange for half the royalties for seven years. Again, the Royalty Share Plus option involves an exclusivity agreement that requires the book to be on the platform for seven years. But this option allows rights holders to save money upfront by working with premium narrators and sharing royalties.

Though I have not tried the Royalty Share Plus program, I can assure you it's not an option I feel is worth pursuing. If you can swing the higher premium, go all the way and get a narrator for their full PFH. Then you can own the distribution rights outright.

Like the 50/50 royalty split, the Royalty Share Plus program can only be terminated with permission from the narrator. Again, you must contact ACX Support to break the contract and delist the title. Then, you'll need to republish the title with the new distribution rights agreement. It's a lot more heartache and hassle than I'd recommend. Avoid this option if you can.

HOW TO PUBLISH A BOOK ON ACX

Once you set up your free ACX account and enter all relevant tax and bank info, you can then add your title. Log in and select **Add Your Title** in the top right corner of the window. Next, you must find your title. Here's the tricky part. If you don't have your print book or ebook currently published, then hold off. ACX requires a live ebook or print book on Amazon in order to publish an audiobook.

SECTION 4: PUBLISH

You must have one or the other to move forward.

Now, search for your book with the title or author's name. Once you find it, select **This is My Book**. A pop-up will prompt you with two choices:

1. I'm looking for someone to narrate and produce my audiobook.
2. I already have audio files for this book, and I want to sell it.

If you produced your audiobook, you'll select the latter option. For most newbies, the first option works best. You'll iron out the selection process in the next few steps. Click **Continue**. If you select the first choice, you can skim the next few instructions. For the rest of you, let's keep moving.

Read through the detailed *ACX Book Posting Agreement*. Though I'd love to cover all the options in the agreement, it'd be impossible to do so without forgetting one element or the other. Please read through it and if you have questions, contact the ACX Support Team for clarification.

Once you're set scrolling through their legalese, check the box next to *I have read the above ACX Book Posting Agreement and agree to its terms*. Now, select **Agree and Continue**.

The book description associated with your title on Amazon should appear in the first box. If the book description doesn't appear, type or paste it into this spot. ACX descriptions do not have the same robust support KDP books have. What you see is what you get.

Next, enter the copyright information, including the print copyright owner, the print copyright year, and the audiobook copyright owner.

You'll most likely list your name or the business entity you use to publish your content.

Now choose whether your book is fiction or nonfiction, and then select the best category suited to your audiobook. You won't have too many choices here, so select what fits best.

In the next option, you'll select if you want to receive auditions from potential narrators. Since you're new, I recommend accepting auditions. It's a fun process to see different interpretations of your work from various voice-over talents. Once your book lists to ACX, you'll see auditions within one day to a week. How many auditions you receive depends on how enticing your content is and the niche you're in.

In the event you have a narrator already, you can select the negative option and move on. I'll share more about how to find and select a narrator in the following subchapter.

Next you can select the type of narration you prefer. Narrow your preference down to:

- Gender—stick with the same gender as the author/character for continuity in voice
- Language
- Accent—choose this based on the author's dialect or the main character's voice should you need a specific accent
- Voice age
- Vocal style

Once you have your narrator preferences dialed in, you can now provide other comments or context for your audiobook. Here's the part where you need to pull out all stops and share a little about yourself, your plans, and how you see your audiobook performing.

Next, you must select two to three pages of your best content for the narrator auditions. Don't go easy on them! Make sure you get the juiciest part of your book, so you can see what they're made of in each audition. Attach any additional notes and directions you have for the narrator in the empty box. Then upload the sample manuscript for auditions as a Word document, PDF, or TXT file. You won't need anything fancy.

Once you upload the document, click **Continue**.

You'll get a prompt to upload your Table of Contents. ACX will set up all your chapter titles, so it will be easier for your narrator to upload the audio files in the right order. If you produced your audiobook on your own, you'll upload the audio files in the next step.

Fill out the approximate word count for your manuscript. Before you do that, it's a good idea to remove any content you may not want read from the file. If you want the narrator to read it in the audiobook, then leave it in the manuscript. If you don't want them to read your entire resources page or your special thanks, remove the content before confirming your final word count. Also, save the narrator-specific manuscript with only the content you want them to read as a separate file someplace you can easily access. This will save a lot of time and heartache for everyone involved.

For territory rights, choose **World**. The only time you wouldn't select this option is if you don't own the copyright or if you have sold the distribution rights for a specific region.

EXCLUSIVE VS NON-EXCLUSIVE DISTRIBUTION

Pay close attention to this step in the audiobook publishing process. Both avenues come with their share of pros and cons.

Exclusive distribution gives you a 40% royalty of every sale, which roughly equates to forty cents of every dollar. Should you choose to be exclusive to ACX, you cannot distribute your audiobook anywhere else. The term of this exclusive agreement is seven years, though you can terminate the agreement ninety days after publishing the audiobook. In the event you want out of the agreement, contact ACX Support. As mentioned previously, royalty splits are always exclusive. Breaking an exclusive agreement with the cooperation of your narrator is a bit of a headache, so again, choose this option wisely.

For ACX exclusive audiobooks, you will receive up to 100 promotional codes to share with reviewers in the U.S. and U.K. After release, you'll receive twenty-five codes per region. Once you use at least ten codes, you can ask for more. These codes have no monetary value and are merely provided for building buzz around your audiobook and getting reviews.

For non-exclusive distribution, you earn 25% of every sale, equating to about twenty-five cents out of every dollar. Non-exclusive distribution is for those who want their audiobook on more platforms. Sadly, under the non-exclusive option, you will not get promotional codes for your audiobook. We will explore another option later that provides the equivalent option for a competing retailer.

There are several other audiobook platforms worth considering beyond ACX. The ACX exclusivity agreement prevents distribution to libraries and other audiobook marketplaces. If you want to publish your audiobook through other mediums (i.e., video, CDs, etc.), then non-exclusive will be your only choice.

SELECTING YOUR TYPE OF PRODUCTION

We have covered the types of agreements you might execute with narrators. After you choose the type of distribution, you'll need to choose the type of production that best fits your needs. Choosing **Pay for Production** gives you the option to select paying for the narration per finished hour (PFH). Use the drop-down to select the range that best suits your budget. Keep in mind, many narrators can negotiate, while some have to abide by union-set wages. If a narrator won't negotiate with you, don't sweat it.

In the second box, you can select the royalty share option. When you select both boxes, you agree to the Royalty Share Plus model, where you pay a lower PFH in exchange for half the net profits for the next seven years.

Select an option and then hit **Save and Continue**.

POSTING TO ACX

The last screen confirms your audiobook metadata. Should you need to make any changes, do so now by clicking **Edit Retail Information**. Otherwise, select **Post to ACX**.

Once this is done, you just wait for the auditions to come in. ACX usually emails once you have an audition. Pop into your account once per week to review them. When you hear a good audition, contact the narrator, and strike up a conversation. Figure out if you need to arrange a PFH deal, a royalty split, or a combination of both.

Sometimes you will not have to make a payment upfront; however, most narrators prefer a down payment to begin work. After all, they have to pay their bills, and producing your audiobook doesn't come free. Just make sure you keep all your communication with the narrator on the ACX platform. Confirm all payments through ACX direct messaging, so you have trackable communication should anything go wrong.

After the narrator completes the project and uploads it to ACX, it'll be up to you to arrange payment. If you agreed to the royalty share, you pay nothing.

HOW TO FIND A NARRATOR ON ACX

Once you decide to produce an audiobook, it's a good idea to research your options for narrators. Though you can add your title to ACX and accept auditions from narrators, it's always a good idea to find the narrator who best suits your needs. Then you won't have to kiss too many frogs before you find your one prince.

Though you can skip to this step before you upload your audiobook, I wouldn't recommend it. Having a project ready ahead of time is a good idea when you break ground with potential narrators. You appear more organized and professional when you have your project available for a quick review.

To find a narrator, go to the main ACX.com landing page. Hover over **Search** in the top right corner, then select **Producers for Hire**. You'll find the entire list of narrators along with samples of their work. Narrow down the choices using the **Filters** option on the left side.

Skip to compensation and narrow down how much you're willing to pay PFH. Also, select **Royalty Share** or **Royalty Share Plus** if applicable. Click **Apply** and you'll see the options will decrease significantly. Now, go through the other selections to narrow down your field even further, including:

1. Genre—what type of book did you write?
2. Gender of narrator
3. Language spoken
4. Accent—if needed
5. Vocal style
6. Voice age
7. Location—though this may not be as important, selecting a location might reveal something about your narrator's environment and style.
8. Audible Approved—ACX deems these narrators to be the cream of the crop. Expect to pay a higher premium for their services.

Trim down your selections, then review the audio samples. When you find a narrator you like, click on their name to view their profile. Once on their profile, you'll see a picture and some facts about them, including:

- A brief bio
- Gender
- Location
- Website
- Per finished hour rates
- More audiobook samples

- Anything relevant to their background as a narrator

Assuming you find a good fit, click the **Send Message** button. Give the narrator all the details they need to know about your book, including the PFH, the length, and any expectations you have. Remember, despite how close you might feel to the narrator, keep all your dialogue on the ACX platform. In case anything goes south between you two, you'll always have a record of your communications to fall back on. Of course that means you should keep your communications professional and on point at all times.

Now just sit back and wait for a reply. Don't use the option to make an offer unless the narrator agrees to it in advance. You can only make an offer once every few days, so you don't want to blow this opportunity on a narrator who may or may not be responsive on ACX. Believe it or not, some narrators have profiles on ACX yet never check them. That's why you shouldn't bother to make an offer until you know your narrator is onboard.

WHAT COMES NEXT ON ACX?

Once you have a narrator you like and they're ready to do business, you can get started! You'll have an option to make an offer to the narrator. Give them one to three days to accept it. Should the narrator decline or not respond, you can make another offer to a different narrator. If the narrator agrees to your offer, you must sign a contract to begin.

Sometimes offers will fall through because of your budgeted time. As you communicate with your narrator, ask for a realistic timeline for them to complete the audiobook. Once the deadline is set, you can build an offer that best suits the narrator's schedule. Included in the timeline are two important areas: the first fifteen minutes and the deadline.

When the first fifteen minutes are complete of the rough draft, your narrator will provide you with a file that demonstrates the progress they are making on the project. You will rarely receive a finished product at this point; at this stage, the first fifteen minutes will give you a rough understanding of how well the narrator is reading your work. Before you approve the first fifteen minutes, review the audio content.

Use over-the-ear headphones to review your audiobook, not earbuds or speakers. Headphones enhance the audiobook experience, making slight differences more noticeable. Pull out your manuscript and follow along with the narration. Listen closely for:

- Mispronunciations
- Extraneous noises
- Missing words or passages

Remember, this is your book, so you don't want the product to sound inferior or below your expectations. Now is the time to be nitpicky. Once you approve the first fifteen minutes, you're officially locked into your agreement with the narrator.

Should you find the first fifteen minutes isn't quite working out as planned, you can always ask to end the relationship. Get in touch with the narrator, express your concerns, and part ways amicably. You both will need to reach out to ACX Support to end the contract so you can find a new narrator.

If you did your research, then chances are pretty likely nothing should go wrong. You will rarely have to break a contract as a result of the narrator's failure to meet your expectations. Just keep your communication open and honest while showing professionalism and respect.

After you approve the first fifteen minutes, sit back and wait. Depending on how large the project is or how far out the deadline is, check in with your narrator occasionally. You don't want to badger or bother your narrator too much. Follow up with them and offer any help where needed.

Once your narrator completes the project and uploads it to your dashboard, you'll get an email notification to review the content. Similar to the first fifteen minutes, review the audiobook content. Note any issues or discrepancies. I recommend including the chapter title and timestamp indicating where you find any issues. It's better for you to address the issues now than for a listener to leave a bad review.

When you're ready to send the audiobook to market, click **Approve for Sale**. ACX will prompt you with a confirmation pop-up. Include the rights holder name and year, then click **Confirm**. An automated email and message will go out, confirming your approval for sale. Now the audiobook will be reviewed by ACX's Quality Control Team to make sure everything is up to specs.

Within a couple of months, ACX will let you know if they approve your audiobook for sale. Should there be any issues, they'll let you know. Send all the issues to your narrator to fix. Go back through the earlier steps again. Once ACX approves your audio files, your audiobook will automatically publish to Amazon, Audible, and iTunes.

What if you don't want to limit yourself to those three audiobook retail platforms? Then you need to look into another viable option called Findaway Voices.

FINDAWAY VOICES

Founded in 2016, Findaway Voices is an publishing platform for downloadable audiobooks. Though relatively new to the self-publishing industry, the parent company Findaway has been around since 2006. Findaway produces a wide range of audiobooks, from traditional to interactive formats. When the platform launched, they only had a handful of distribution options. Over the past few years, they have developed extensive options for authors.

Most recently, the online audio streaming juggernaut Spotify bought Findaway for an estimated $119 million. This could be good or bad for authors. Time will tell since the acquisition happened in early 2022.[xiv]

Unlike ACX, Findaway Voices distributes to nearly forty different retailers as well as libraries. They don't require exclusivity and pay an 80% royalty. There's a small catch though—you get eighty cents out of every dollar of *net* profits.

Findaway Voices charges nothing upfront for distribution, instead opting to collect 20% of your net profits. They don't make money if you don't make money. Remember, based on where your sales originate, you'll only get 80% of each sale after the retailer collects their cut.

For example, Findaway Voices has an agreement with Apple iTunes to get 45% of each sale. Once the sale is made, Apple takes 55%

of the total sales price. Then, Findaway Voices splits the remaining 45% with you as follows: 20% to Findaway and you earn 80%.

According to some insiders,[xv] ACX has an agreement to take 25% to 40% of every sale through Apple iTunes. If you're exclusive to ACX, then you get 40% of every sale made through Apple. Anyone who is non-exclusive gets 25% of every sale through Apple. It's not a huge upgrade moving to Findaway Voices, but one thing you get there that you don't get with ACX is the ability to set your pricing. Of course, that's not the only perk of Findaway Voices.

They also provide 100 promotional codes to build buzz around your audiobook and get book reviews. The codes carry no monetary value and merely function as a promotional tool, but don't underestimate the power of these codes. ACX offers 100 promo codes only in the U.S. and U.K., but Findaway Voices offers codes in more regions through Spotify.

The next biggest advantage to publishing through Findaway Voices is getting distribution to libraries. ACX doesn't offer library distribution, which limits your reach to listeners who don't buy audiobooks. Rather than limiting your reach to only some listeners, you open yourself up to a wider audience with library distribution.

Earning money through libraries is more complex. Some libraries will buy a copy of your book for up to two to three times the suggested retail price. Then, there's a pay-per-checkout model, where you'll be paid when someone checks out your book. You'll earn a percentage of a global pool of money from the library checkout system. Refer to the Findaway Voices Help section for further details (DaleLinks.com/FindawayHelp).

The biggest and best advantage to producing an audiobook through Findaway Voices is the ability to price your audiobook. ACX automatically prices your content based on the length. Even though you can price your ebook and print book how you want, you have no say on how much your book costs through ACX. I think that sucks!

Findaway Voices allows you to price your audiobook whatever you want. If you want to price it bargain-basement low, then you can do it. Do you want to price it super high? Knock yourself out. You can even set a different price for your audiobook if it's distributed through the library system. Remember, when a library buys your book, it's possible that many listeners will check it out, so you may want to make it worth your while and price it higher.

HIRING NARRATORS FOR FINDAWAY VOICES

In late 2023, Findaway Voices shutdown their Marketplace. That means rights holders can no longer use the Findaway platform to find qualified narrators. If you distribute on Findaway Voices, you'll need audio files prepped and ready to publish. If you are looking for trusted narration services, check out ALLi's Watchdog List (DaleLinks.com/Watchdog). Search "audiobook" to get recommended service providers.

If ACX and Findaway Voices don't work for you, or if you want more distribution options, there are other ways to distribute audiobooks.

MISCELLANEOUS AUDIOBOOK DISTRIBUTION

I could spend an entire book discussing audiobook distribution, but I'll keep it brief and stick to what you need to know. Audiobook distribution doesn't live and die by ACX or Findaway Voices. If your mission is to reach more readers, then explore other avenues beyond these two big distributors.

Here is a short list of audiobook distributors to consider:

- Author's Republic
- PublishDrive
- Audiobooks Unleashed
- Lantern Audio
- XinXii

Don't spread yourself too thin as a newbie author. Consider other options beyond downloadable digital content. Diversifying your author earnings can provide stability if your regular income sources aren't sufficient. Should you publish audiobooks before ebooks or print books? No, but that's because I believe you're already spinning several plates. Choose your battles wisely and avoid overloading yourself on every potential avenue possible.

Maybe come back to this option once your first book is on the market. If your budget permits, hire someone to handle it for you and then continue marketing and promoting your upcoming book launch. That leads me to why publishing wide may not be the best option for newbies.

PUBLISHING WIDE – WHY NEWBIES SHOULD AVOID THIS

The modern-day self-publishing model is a far cry from what it used to be. In late 2007, KDP disrupted the market and created higher expectations for accessibility. Since then, several new self-publishing platforms emerged, giving indie authors a chance to reach a larger audience. Enter "publishing wide."

You'll often hear indie authors talk about "going wide" or "publishing wide." This refers to publishing your title beyond KDP alone. Though KDP is a fantastic option for newbies, it shouldn't be the only option for their entire career. Yes, you can make a substantial income through KDP, and many authors continue to remain exclusive and often loyal to the distribution platform. The issue lies in the two-way relationship with Amazon.

Amazon isn't your friend. Sorry to break the news to you, but they can and will terminate your account with no just cause and recourse. While the chances of your account being terminated are unlikely as long as you play by the rules, there's still a chance it can happen. Your odds of running afoul of KDP are slim as a new author, but you don't want to play with fire.

For new authors, stick to publishing through KDP and ACX. Once you understand the fundamentals of self-publishing through KDP, then you can look into other avenues. It's hard enough to write, edit, format, distribute, and market your book, so don't make it even harder by trying to figure out multiple platforms.

Once you break into the business and see the inner workings of publishing to Amazon KDP, then consider other options like:

- Apple Books
- Barnes & Noble Press
- Kobo
- Google Play Books

Also, think about using other distributors like:

- Draft2Digital
- PublishDrive
- Lulu
- IngramSpark
- Streetlib
- Bookvault
- And more!

There's never going to be a perfect time to publish wide. You'll simply know when you're ready based on your comfort level. Most coaching clients I've worked with over the years were usually ready to publish wide after their first year in the business. One year gave them enough time to figure things out, including keyword research and developing a solid marketing strategy.

PUBLISHING BEYOND AMAZON

Once you're ready to venture into publishing wide, take an inventory of your current backlog of books. This means auditing all three iterations of print, electronic, and audio. Most print books aren't in exclusive publishing programs, so you're good to publish wide.

As far as ebooks are concerned, make sure your ebook is not in the KDP Select Program. The ninety-day exclusivity agreement bars you from publishing that ebook to other online distributors. I wouldn't recommend testing Amazon on this since they have systems crawling the internet to discover any violations of their policies. Indie author Derek Murphy accidentally triggered the KDP system when he missed one small, obscure platform.[xvi]

He published his book wide but returned to an exclusive deal with

KDP Select. Though Derek believed he had removed his book from all marketplaces beyond Amazon KDP, he missed one. Amazon penalized Derek immediately after discovering the unknown distributor of his ebook when he joined KDP Select. Though KDP didn't close his account, Derek could not use KDP Select for over a year, and I'm sure he had a red mark on his record.

When you publish wide, be sure your ebook isn't in KDP Select and the ninety-day period has lapsed. Select the **Promote and Advertise** button, then look under the **KDP Select** box. That will show you when the book's enrollment starts and ends. To deselect enrollment, click the **Manage KDP Select Enrollment** option, then deselect the box. Again, you must fulfill the full term before publishing wide.

With ACX, you can pull out of the exclusivity agreement only if you fulfilled the audiobook through a per-finished-hour agreement. You can only ask to get out of the exclusivity agreement ninety days after your title first went on sale. Anyone with royalty splits cannot remove their title from exclusivity until the seven-year agreement is up. The exception to royalty splits is if you get consent from the narrator after the initial ninety days.

If you want to reverse your decision and go back to publishing exclusively with KDP, you have to take a few extra steps. First, you must remove your title from distribution on all other platforms. Next, confirm your title is no longer available through those avenues. It can take upwards of six to eight weeks for some platforms to catch up. Last, you simply go back into your KDP Dashboard and enroll your ebook back in KDP Select.

Choosing enrollment is instantaneous, so your ebook will be in the program immediately. I don't have enough experience with audiobook distribution to speak about going back to exclusive with ACX. I'm sure the process would work the same in that you'd reach out to ACX Support and request the exclusivity agreement. Remember, once you do, you're committed for at least the next seven years or sometimes ninety days before you can opt out again.

No matter the publishing type, publishing wide is a bit too much for new authors. For now, I recommend keeping it simple. Don't make matters more complicated. When you feel you've gotten the system down pat and you're earning enough revenue to give it a shot, then you can consider publishing wide. For now, stick to the basics.

SECTION 5: THE HIDDEN COSTS OF SELF-PUBLISHING

I've heard many heartbreaking stories about aspiring authors who sunk their life savings into their book only to have little to no return. It sucks, and I never grow immune to feeling a deep level of empathy for them. After all, you pour your heart and soul into your book, so when you put all you have into it and don't see a return, it's more than gut-wrenching.

Self-publishing is tough and unforgiving, regardless of what experts or gurus say. You can invest all your time, energy, attention, and money into it only to have nothing to show for it. I never recommend you believe you're going to be the one exception to the rule.

The harsh reality is self-publishing should be a hobby for your first few years in the business. Continue to work your day job so you can pay your bills. Don't neglect time with your family, because you need them when times get tough in this business. The most important rule of all lies in how you invest in your work.

Never spend money you aren't willing to lose.

Let's shout that out again so the people in the back of the room hear it! Do *not* spend any money you cannot afford to lose. Far too many writers romanticize this business to a point where they become nearly delusional about their future level of success. Many authors who self-publish have high hopes for their books, but they don't do as well as expected.

I've seen aspiring authors and self-publishers who thought they had the secret to success in this industry. No one thing will make your business explode or your book become a tremendous success. Once you understand that, you'll then be able to invest in your book wisely and with no unrealistic expectations.

Despite the risks and potential losses, let's discuss the costs of self-publishing your book. Keep in mind these are not hard-and-fast rules. You might have a specific skill set or connection that could mitigate some of these costs. While I encourage managing most duties yourself if you have more time than money, I still recommend hiring out when you can afford it. There's no sense spinning your wheels needlessly for hours when a pro can do what you need in a fraction of the time. You don't want to work on your 50,000-word manuscript for the next five years because you're trying to do it all yourself. Sometimes, you have to know when to do it yourself and when to find someone more qualified to do it for you.

For example, when I broke into the business in 2014, I designed all my own covers. When I realized my covers were subpar and I didn't have the skills to make better ones, I resigned myself to hiring professional cover designers. My biggest issue, though, was that I didn't have the money.

What I did was take on a little extra freelance work on the side to subsidize my book cover designs. Though I didn't prefer working outside of writing and publishing, I was realistic. If I kept making my own covers, I wouldn't make any substantial living in this business.

While you've already learned the value and costs of hiring an editor, let's look at other potential expenses associated with self-publishing your book. As you read this, think about ways to leverage any disposable income you have now to hire professionals. Should you not have extra income, you need to think of ways you can either do it yourself or come up with the funds to hire. Again, I lean heavily in favor of hiring a pro, but only if you have the means and you're comfortable parting ways with the money.

To avoid redundancy, I'll cover costs I haven't already discussed in previous chapters. For instance, I've covered the cost of editors and audiobook narrators. There are many other miscellaneous costs that can and will chip away at your finances. I'll start with the most important expenses and work my way to the least important items to consider. That's not to say the expense isn't worth it, but some of the items on my list are less important or even optional for newbie authors.

PRODUCING THE PACKAGING

All consumers judge a book by its cover, which holds true not just from an exterior standpoint but also from the interior. Remember, readers are paying their hard-earned money to read your content. Sure, having your content edited is a start, but now you need to entertain the eyes with a dazzling interior. I don't expect you to have next-level photography in your book if you're publishing a romance novel. Nor do I think you need to have the same simple layout that might work in fiction inside a nonfiction book.

You need to be acutely aware of what your reading audience expects in your niche and adjust accordingly. This holds true for both the cover and interior design. Get these two elements right, and you'll not only get quite a few buyers, but you'll have more happy readers.

COVER DESIGN COSTS

Hiring an experienced cover designer doesn't have to cost much. While authors like me or Chris Fox spend upwards of $1,000 for cover design, you don't have to invest nearly that much. For Chris, he has computer-digital illustration to match his niche, so the investment makes sense for his needs. Also, Chris has the readership and a budget for these expenses. The same goes for me. I have enough income to justify the expense, so I can spend $800 on a cover design.

Back in 2014, I didn't have that type of money. So I hired cover designers through the online freelance platform Fiverr. Remember my previous story about creating my cover only to discover the original Fiverr cover performed better? That is an example of how a cover doesn't have to cost a lot to be effective. Should your book cover not be quite what you want it to be, remember you can replace it later when you can afford the investment.

Book cover designs can cost anywhere from about $7 to $1,500, depending on the book cover designer's level of detail and experience. In my YouTube video *I Paid 5 Designers on Fiverr To Design the Same Cover*, viewers got to see creations ranging from $35 to $800. The viewers seemed split in their votes. Half the people voted for the premium cover gig, while the other half voted for the cheapest gig. The cheaper gig simply didn't have what I was looking for, though I appreciated the cover design.

When you're ordering a cover design, you must account for the cost for all three publication iterations in print, ebook, and audiobook.

SECTION 5: THE HIDDEN COSTS OF SELF-PUBLISHING

Even if you don't plan to publish a specific type, keep the cost in mind just in case.

Ebook and audiobook covers cost less than print covers. If you're cash-strapped, you can always use your ebook cover for your print book's front cover. Then you can draft your own full wrap from the ebook version without paying the higher cost for a separate design that includes the full spine and back. You'll find several tutorials on my YouTube channel showing how easy it is. Just remember, doing it yourself isn't always going to mean you'll have the best-looking print book cover.

As a reminder, for the audiobook cover, avoid stretching your ebook cover to fit the square dimensions. I used to stretch my ebook covers to make audiobook covers, and they didn't look very professional. My audiobook sales suffered until I had a cover custom-made for audiobooks. It's a worthy investment, so don't skimp here.

To publish different versions of your book, such as hardback or coil bound, you'll need a separate cover. All covers are not equal, so you can't simply use the same cover across all iterations. You need to account for these additional costs. Sometimes, book cover designers may not be aware of a particular format and may charge more based on the difficulty.

Some book cover designers will charge a premium to package all cover iterations. Most of the time, that'll include the ebook, print book, and audiobook cover. For example, when I order my covers through my previous designers Marko, he had a premium option where he designs the:

- ebook cover
- print cover—paperback, hardback, or hardback with jacket

(not all three)
- audiobook cover
- five social media assets for promotion
- four book renderings in 3D

I'm able to get all those assets in a bundle and save a lot more money. When you create the packaging for your book, consider everything you might need to launch and promote your book. It'll save you a lot of hassle.

INTERIOR FORMATTING

Back in 2014, I did all my interior formatting with Microsoft Word. The sales were minor at first. Once I started gaining traction as an author, the time spent figuring out how to format paid off. Sadly, looking back on those books, I can see that the formatting was barely passable. Could I hire a designer to redo the interiors? Sure, but will I? No, since I'm focusing on pushing my brand forward. If I had to do it all over again, I would've hired a professional interior formatter, also known as a typesetter.

Microsoft Word is sufficient for writing and publishing your manuscript. After all, you only need a .doc or .docx for uploading to most platforms. However, as we covered earlier, I recommend formatting to .epub.

If you want to design an .epub yourself, you can use premium software like Scrivener, Vellum, Atticus, and more. The software can cost $100 or more and some of them have a steep learning curve. Draft2Digital offers a free interior formatting service for fiction and nonfiction books without many interior images. It's more than sufficient and doesn't cost a dime.

SECTION 5: THE HIDDEN COSTS OF SELF-PUBLISHING

There are two types of ebook formatting: fixed layout and reflowable content. With a fixed layout, you're creating a document you can't change. Similar to a print book, the text and image layout will always be the same. Whereas with reflowable content, the reader has control of the font type, size, and overall layout. Reflowable layouts are more flexible for the reader and are especially helpful when reading on various devices.

I recommend you format your ebook with reflowable content. KDP even rewards some books for having a reflowable layout through programs like *Great on Kindle*. A fixed layout can cause some friction across devices but might be necessary if you have a specific look you want to achieve.

When using a reflowable layout, you'll discover it doesn't quite appear like your original document. KDP will automatically format the interior so the content adjusts according to the device. If you upload a .doc, .docx, or .pdf, KDP will adjust the interior. Those file types will be formatted by KDP to an .epub file so it's readable on all Kindles.

Don't worry when you see your photo isn't in the right place or your text isn't quite in the same position you set it. Once your ebook launches, I highly recommend buying a copy and reading it across multiple devices. Use your computer, phone, and any e-reader to see how it looks. Play with the font type, font size, and overall layout functions of the device you're on. Proofing your content doesn't just apply to print books. You need to look at your product in all its iterations so you're intimately aware of what your readers see.

HIRING AN INTERIOR FORMATTER

Interior formatting costs vary from one source to the next. You can find freelancers on Fiverr who'll design your interior for as low as $5. For more premium services, you can expect to pay upwards of $1000. Again, similar to book covers, how detailed your interior is and how many pages you have are relevant to how much the provider will charge.

Before plunking down lots of money on a typesetter, hire them for a test run. Give them a few pages to work with and see how well they understand your directions. Some typesetters may just do the basics while others might deliver detailed interiors. Regardless of what you choose, hire a typesetter based on your budget and how well they design according to your expectations.

For most newbie authors, I recommend sticking to a "less is more" philosophy. Rather than investing too much in your first book, it's a better idea to start low. New authors shouldn't spend thousands on their first book. Heck, even spending hundreds is a stretch. If you have discretionary expenses, allocate those funds towards editing, cover design, or marketing. In due time, you'll afford more intricate interiors.

ORDERING PROOFS

One of the biggest rules in publishing is you should always own a single copy of every book, including each of the various iterations. Don't simply trust the platform to get it right, because sometimes they'll get it wrong. You'll find it's better you discover minor discrepancies and errors in your book rather than a reader. Once a reader finds those issues, all bets are off. You'll either have:

- An angry customer who leaves a bad review
- A reader who'll never buy another book
- A hater who'll shout from the mountain tops how you're the worst

After you publish your ebook, immediately order a proof copy. Visit your Amazon product page and buy it. However you priced your book is how much it'll cost. Now, don't sweat it. You aren't violating any terms of service, and it's completely allowed. Can you simply use the previewer in the KDP dashboard? Sure, but it won't be the same experience as actually downloading it on your device. As mentioned previously, view your ebook across a few different devices and scroll through your content. You don't need to spend the time re-reading your book for the fifty-millionth time. Just flip through it.

Now, experiment with the font size, font type, and layout preferences. If you're using a mobile device, read it in landscape and portrait mode (sideways or upright). Any way you can read it, give it a go so you have an intimate understanding of the customer experience.

Should you find any issues, make the corrections, upload an updated manuscript to KDP, and click the **Publish** button. You don't have to delist or unpublish a book based on a minor error. Of course, the same holds true for print and audiobooks.

As mentioned in a previous chapter, you get the option of ordering proofs in the last step of publishing. From my experience, it's much easier to order a proof copy through Amazon, especially if you have Prime.

My biggest gripe with KDP is when ordering wholesale copies. You can't use your Prime membership so you pay additional shipping costs, and the delivery takes much longer than normal. I'd rather skip the wholesale cost and buy directly from the site to get the print book faster. Much like the ebook, when you purchase a print book from Amazon, you will see the sale in your dashboard and earn royalties for the sale.

What may surprise you is that whether you order wholesale author copies or buy from Amazon, the cost is about the same. Just don't abuse the system when buying a proof copy. One copy is fine, but beyond that, you should probably order author copies in bulk. I discourage ordering too many copies on Amazon because when you purchase a copy, it will influence your bestseller rank. Rather than getting caught gaming the system—accidentally or on purpose—err on the side of caution.

Once you receive your proof copy, take your time proofing the content. KDP and other printers can get things wrong. Be mindful of this issue and never skip the proofing process.

Not too long ago, a friend visited from out of town, and he flipped through a proof copy of my book *Secrets of a Permafree Book*. Though the book came from IngramSpark, it had one rather large flaw. The printer mistakenly printed the interior twice! Thinking back, I realized I'd nonchalantly flipped through the interior and assumed all was well. Most readers may not care about getting a twice-printed book, but a select few readers will view it as amateur hour.

Don't do what I did. When you order your print proof, go through every page and pay close attention to the layout and typesetting. Though you may have gotten the interior right, the printer might have gotten it wrong. Rather than allowing your readers to discover the issue, it's best that you find it first.

In instances like mine, I determined the misprint was a one-off issue and not every copy had the error. That's the price you pay for print-on-demand. The system isn't perfect, and human beings are at the helm of the operation. While machines and technology rarely make mistakes, humans will. Thoroughly proof your print books.

Again, should you find any issues, first review the interior you uploaded to the platform to ensure you weren't the cause of the mistakes. Once you eliminate yourself as the offender, move onto the distributor. For KDP, scroll down and click the **Contact Us** feature in your dashboard. Get a representative on the phone if you can. Otherwise, lean on live Chat Support or Email Support.

Find out what went wrong on their end of the production. If it's simply a one-off mistake, then you can request an additional proof and move on. However, in some extenuating circumstances, you might find the print team created some type of formatting issue on their end. Ask when you can expect to have the issue resolved and request a notification when all is well. Any time KDP or IngramSpark improperly prints a proof, I request a replacement or refund. They always send a replacement.

INGRAMSPARK PRINT PROOFS

Unlike KDP, IngramSpark allows you to order a proof copy before publishing without a watermark. The unfortunate part of it is the fulfillment process is a little long and overpriced. A proof copy will cost the same as retail with the shipping included. For standard shipping, your book will get to you in about two weeks. For expedited shipping, you pay significantly more.

Plan ahead when publishing to IngramSpark so you don't have additional costs or excessive time added to the process.

AUDIOBOOK PROOFS

When publishing your audiobook, you must get an audiobook proof. If you went through the entire process of producing the audiobook, it might be a pain to listen to the book again. You should still do it. Listen to the audiobook at 2x speed so you can move quickly through the content. Look for any accidental bloopers or outtakes. When you find a mistake, figure out a way to fix the issue with your narrator. After that, the narrator or you can upload the corrected audio file.

ACX provides complimentary promo codes for exclusive distribution, and you should use one of those to listen to your own book. Findaway Voices provides the same service, so again, download the audiobook and listen to it in its entirety.

Ordering proofs is a critical step in the publishing process—one you shouldn't skip. It won't cost you a dime for audiobooks, but for ebooks and print books, it can run about how much you charge per copy. Build that expense into your publishing budget so you catch any issues missed on the previous passes. The benefit to owning your content is sharing it with friends, family, and even connections. You can then always carry a copy to share with others and build more awareness of your work.

MARKETING & PROMOTION

Woo! This chapter is going to be absurdly short, and for good reason. Marketing and promotion are never-ending necessities in this business. Without them, you're doomed to languish in obscurity while praying someone, anyone, will discover your content. You're in a pay-to-play world. If you aren't investing in some type of marketing and promotion for your book, you're at a greater disadvantage than most authors.

I can't give any specific numbers or tell you how much to invest in your marketing and promotion. Heck, the savvy self-publisher knows ways to promote their book on a dime. That's what I encourage newbie authors to do—promote more, spend less. Until you bring in a significant income, it's not practical to spend thousands of dollars with the expectation of selling more books.

To promote your book, the best way to gain any traction is by becoming more visible. Get more interviews, host a YouTube channel, write a guest blog post, arrange a local book club, or do anything that tells the world you're an author. Your only limits are your imagination and comfort level.

There's no neon sign flashing above your latest book. You must draw attention to and build awareness around your publication. It's nobody else's responsibility but yours. If you see no book sales, then guess whose fault that is? Yours! The only way to solve that is through marketing and promotion.

In *Promotional Strategies for Books*, I cover a number of sound and proven marketing strategies. Review that book to find out the true value of marketing and promotion. Discover just how simple it can be as a new author.

Much like I shared earlier in this book, invest no money you can't stand to lose. This especially holds true for marketing and promotion. Though you might have one author who swears by Facebook Ads, you might not get the same results for your book. I could say the same with Bookbub Ads. Some authors crush it on the ads platform while others flush their money away.

Should you plan to invest in any marketing and promotion through paid advertising, start low and scale slow. The initial money you invest into paid ads isn't to sell more books but more to learn the system. Once you have a grasp of the system, you can increase your budget. When you find one method that works, double down on it and increase your budget for that avenue. Conversely, if it isn't working, analyze why it didn't work and what you could possibly do to get better results.

It's ridiculous for authors to spend a lot on advertising with no experience or proof of success. These authors are too busy being in love with their work and romanticizing the possibilities that they miss the harsh reality. Paid advertising is for pros who only invest what they can stand to lose and do so with a bit of experience.

Only a fool believes they have the next *Harry Potter* series while blindly throwing money into paid advertising. Money doesn't solve the problem if you don't know how to work the solution properly. Don't become so obsessed with your work that you make risky financial decisions. Almost all authors struggle in this business. Marketing and promotion are tools to ease or decrease your stress. How you use it is completely up to you. If you're willing to learn the right way to leverage paid advertising, it can pay off in dividends.

MANAGING YOUR EXPENSES

Let's get one thing straight—I am not qualified to dispense advice on money and taxes. I'm going to share some general guidelines that

SECTION 5: THE HIDDEN COSTS OF SELF-PUBLISHING

helped me better manage my money and end up in the black instead of the red, like most authors. While books on managing expenses and taxes exist, it's better to consult professionals for specific questions.

Starting on day one, you absolutely must track all your expenses and earnings. It doesn't matter how you track them so long as it's in one spot in a neat and organized fashion. For me, I use Microsoft Excel spreadsheets and separate my earnings from my expenses. Then, I categorize each expense based on what purpose it served. For instance, if I order a proof copy, I categorize it under "Supplies." When paying for ads, I put the expense under "Promotions."

For all your expenses, track every receipt diligently. All physical receipts go into an envelope for the year. Since most of my receipts come electronically, I store those in my email service and back them up in the cloud every few months.

Rely on a certified public accountant for the best ways for you to track your earnings and expenses. The more proactive you are in tracking, the easier it'll be to:

- Set a budget for future spending
- Report your earnings and expenses for taxes
- Identify where you're losing money
- Pinpoint areas where you're earning the most revenue

Don't rely on memory when it comes to earnings and expenses. I used to do that, but that became a problem when I had to report revenue on my annual taxes. I'd look at a receipt and completely blank out on what I'd purchased. If I'd only taken the time to log the expense immediately, I would've had fewer issues.

Regardless of the region where you live in the world, taxes are inevitable. Since you're publishing to Amazon or other U.S.-based companies, reporting publishing income on your taxes is a requirement. Though I can't tell how it's reported by region, I can say you must answer to the government at some point. Rather than leaving it to chance, connect with a professional about the best way to proceed forward for your unique situation.

Back in 2006, I learned something big from retired professional wrestler and former WWE superstar Lance Storm. He was only 38, but he had budgeted wisely, saved enough money, and retired young to live life on his terms. The biggest tip he gave to all of us was:

It's not about the money you earn, but the money you save.

Lance shared how he saw many of his peers struggling to get out of the wrestling business despite having broken-down bodies. Because of financial mismanagement, these wrestlers had no option but to keep working, even at the expense of their health. Meanwhile, Lance had lived frugally, saved his money, and set aside a quarter of his earnings for taxes. Keep in mind, he had to report taxes in Canada and the United States since he was a Canadian citizen who worked for a U.S.-based company.

Every time Lance paid taxes, he had enough money left over to invest in savings. Following his lead over the past few years, I found the same holds true. When the tax bill comes, I don't have to worry if I can afford it.

I recommend you do the same regardless of where you live or how much you make. Build the discipline of sticking to a budget and socking away 25% of your earnings for taxes. Whether you're earning

$5 or $5,000 per month, treat your paydays exactly the same. If you build the discipline now and stick to it, you'll see a bigger payoff in the long term.

CREATING A BUSINESS ENTITY

Many authors want to know if it's a good idea to start a business or file to incorporate a business entity. This depends on your author goals, your discretionary expenses, your available time for research, and your risk aversion.

The issue with publishing books without a business entity lies in potential liability or if you find yourself involved in litigation. Should someone wish to take you to court over copyright or other issues stemming from your publication, you're going to be in for a world of hurt. Without a business entity, the person can sue you and potentially dip into your personal assets since if liability is determined against you, you'll be the person at fault. If your business entity owns the publication, the person could try suing you, but they are less likely to reach assets outside of the business entity.

To put it simply, filing a business entity and publishing under that name helps place a small barrier of protection between you and your business. Because I cannot give legal or tax advice, I have oversimplified the process here and possibly brushed over so many legalities that any lawyer reading this would throw up in their mouth. That's why I recommend you hire an expert in your local area.

REGISTERING A COPYRIGHT

This is the million-dollar question on my YouTube channel: should I file a copyright for my book? Technically, when you first produce your content, you're entitled to basic copyright protections. The problem arises when you must enforce that copyright or bring someone to court for copyright violation.

The chances of copyright abuse are fairly slim in the self-publishing community, but it happens. Sometimes, you'll find pirates who outright steal your work and sell it online. In that case, a copyright will not be of any use since tracking down the thief will be nearly impossible. For other cases, you'll be able to take the person to court, but you must have your copyright registered ahead of the lawsuit. Otherwise, you're going to be swimming upstream just to state your case. Having a legal copyright helps in lawsuits, but beyond that, they don't serve more than showcasing that you did your part in claiming your work.

If you register your work with the U.S. Copyright Office or regional registration offices, then you safeguard your work and protect your rights. Filing a copyright for your work in the U.S. runs about $45 to $65 per work.[xvii] If you have a series of books or a collection of short stories, you can also file them in bulk and get a discount. The process is fairly intuitive and doesn't require having a lawyer or a representative to help.[xviii]

I believe that registering your copyright is not essential for new authors. Only get it if you need peace of mind. As your book grows in popularity and you're making a significant income, you can always revisit the copyright process. For now, formal filing for copyright is a nice-to-have item.

FILING WITH THE LIBRARY OF CONGRESS

Naturally, once authors mention copyright, they inevitably ask about filing your book with the Library of Congress in the U.S.

The Library of Congress is home of the U.S. Copyright Office and the research arm for the U.S. Congress. Having your title listed in the Library of Congress is a way to lend more credibility to your book and cements its legacy in the annals of American history.

To be clear, I see this as even more of a nice-to-have and completely optional. If you're outside the U.S., it makes even less sense, especially if your readership isn't in the United States. However, if it's your lifelong dream to have your book listed in the Library of Congress, then don't let me stop you. Depending on how you file it, the cost starts around $22 and can increase to $100 or more.

For me, I'll pass. I can spend my money better in other areas. I leave that kind of frivolous spending to traditional publishing houses or authors with deeper pockets.

BRICK & MORTAR DISTRIBUTION

Do you want to get your book into physical bookstores, also known as brick-and-mortar? Then you're going to have to put in a little extra work. Sadly, Amazon KDP boasts that they distribute to bookstores, but this option applies to a select few authors who rake in the lion's share of earnings on the platform. Though the world seems to be on the cusp of buying books strictly online, quite a few brick-and-mortar stores still sell millions of dollars in books. Why would you want to miss out on that?

Now, I'm not trying to sell you on getting placement in bookstores, but you should know a few things before trying to get your book onto their shelves.

Most brick-and-mortar stores don't stock Amazon-published books. Some bookstores view Amazon as a competitor, so you can imagine they're reluctant to stock those books. Some insiders think that using a free ISBN from Amazon eliminates your chances of getting your book in physical stores.

Fellow YouTuber and former coaching student Keith Wheeler proved the theory wrong when he got his books into local bookstores while having a free ISBN from Amazon. Keith did some preparation to get his book into the store, and now he can officially announce that it's available both in physical stores and on Amazon.

There are two ways your book can be sold in a physical bookstore: through IngramSpark distribution or via consignment. If you distribute your book on IngramSpark, you must agree to a few terms before a store will even consider selling your book. According to IngramSpark, bookstores are more likely to select a title if it has:

- Returns enabled
- 55% or more wholesale discount

There are a few issues to consider when using these two options. The main problem is you take all the risks while the bookstore reaps the rewards through profits. That 55% discount comes out of your bottom line. While you make considerably more per sale online, you're taking a huge pay cut with distribution to brick-and-mortar. Is the placement really worth it? You may decide that it is if the bookstore sells your book.

The next issue is in having returns enabled. Unlike Amazon KDP, when a bookstore makes the return, you pay for it. Yes, you didn't read that wrong. When a bookstore orders your books, they pay for the printing costs and slight markup from wholesale. Should they decide to return the book for whatever reason, you pay for the print costs and the shipping. Sometimes, authors choose to have the books destroyed since it's the cheaper alternative.

I heard many horrible scenarios where bookstores have returned hundreds of dollars in books that the author had to pay for. While the bookstore is technically at fault for ordering too many books without knowing if the books would sell, you're the one who'll have to pay the bill.

If you're okay with the risk of taking returns and cutting your profits, then go for it. You'll at least be able to brag when a store stocks your book. Some bookstores will stock your work without the returns enabled and without the deep discount. That's primarily for proven authors or local authors who'll drive traffic and sales.

That's where getting friendly with your local bookstore helps. With Keith, he got to know the local bookstore management and staff. He's an avid reader and frequented the establishment. When it came time to ask for his book to be sold in their store, they didn't even sweat that he had an Amazon imprint. The bookstore staff had come to know and love him, so they offered his book for sale on a consignment deal.

Publishing through IngramSpark would have made it easier for Keith to negotiate with the bookstore for ordering stock. Either way, for Keith, it was a win-win situation. If the bookstore stocks your book on a consignment deal, then you get a percentage of the profits when the book sells. With IngramSpark fulfillment, you'll see the profits in your dashboard as soon as the bookstore places the order.

If you don't get brick-and-mortar distribution, it isn't the end of the world. Quite a few indie authors make a substantial living in this business and have never had a single title in a bookstore. If you're hung up on getting your title into a bookstore without the risk and the upfront work, then just become wildly successful. Then, they will have to stock your books since readers will demand copies.

WEBSITE ORDER FULFILLMENT

Fulfilling orders through your website is nice but not a necessity. You may earn larger profits while building awareness of your brand by selling from your own website instead of Amazon or other retailers. Imagine training your readership to buy directly from you instead of Amazon. You could charge the same amount as Amazon while profiting far more. You could even profit the same amount and discount the cost on your website through unique coupon codes or exclusive links, so your readers can enjoy your content at a lower price.

If you decide to fulfill orders through your website, then you need to consider the costs of:

1. Website hosting—anywhere from $10 to $40 per month.
2. Online Shopping Carts—Shopify, WooCommerce, and other shopping carts run about $0 to $30 per month. Obviously, the cheaper models have fewer features and integrations.
3. Returns—If you have a no-return policy, you won't have the burden of accepting returns and issuing refunds for the books.
4. Payment Processor Fees—if you're using PayPal, Stripe, or other payment processors, anticipate a small fee to be deducted from every sale.

The biggest issues you'll run into are building out the infrastructure, managing the orders, and driving online traffic to your website. It's a lot more work than you think, and is something many indie authors take for granted when publishing through platforms like KDP and IngramSpark.

Think about order management alone. You are responsible for handling all customer returns, complaints, and questions. Before that, you need to make sure your website is well-maintained and runs smoothly on checkout.

These are just a few issues you'll run into with website fulfillment. Before you break into this area, make sure you have the finances to support it. The worst-case scenario is shutting down your website store if it doesn't generate enough money.

Is direct selling necessary for newbie authors? No. Keep your publishing business as simple as possible when starting out. Website fulfillment is a great option for authors who have a following or a way to drive traffic to their site. Beyond that, you're just adding more work to your plate.

REVITALIZING A DEAD BOOK

The day will come when your book falls out of the good graces of the Amazon algorithm or other online retailers. What once worked with your cover design, book description, or keywords won't work as well five or even ten years after launching. Every book has a certain shelf life to it. Be ready to revitalize your book when necessary.

As you see the relevancy and book sales taper off, consider changing one of these elements:

- Book cover
- Book description
- Keywords
- Content
- Marketing and promotional strategies

As we discussed in the section on covers, recovering your book can range from $7 to $1000. If you hire a pro to rewrite your book description, then account for that cost. To replace your keywords, follow the process you learned earlier or get a copy of *Amazon Keywords for Books* for a more detailed guide. Of course, you must test all new marketing campaigns so you can see if they resonate with your readers.

In a worst-case scenario, update your content and create a second edition of your book. This involves adding new material, rewriting old content, and providing new insights that your readers may have missed in the first publication. Since you're creating a new version, consider the costs of editing, proofreading, formatting, and publishing all over again. The second edition is essentially a new book and should be treated accordingly.

When I pivoted my content away from fitness and into self-publishing, I did this for my old books. I went through my backlog, replaced the covers, re-edited the content, cleaned up the ad copy, and fired off a few paid ads. Thankfully, I had already worked with a more cost-effective cover designer to create a newly branded look and feel. After the relaunch, most of the books saw a little more life come back into them.

If you have a book that isn't performing as it should, consider this option. Breathe new life into it and test out different covers, book descriptions, and advertising. When a change gets measurable results, then you know you're headed in the right direction.

CONCLUSION

Anything over $1,000 is a lot of money to invest in any one thing. Self-publishing is no different.

Back when I approached my wife about buying a pallet full of books, I didn't know any better. When I realized I'd never see that money back, I had to come up with an alternative plan that wouldn't cost me a dime. If I planned to invest in anything, I needed a solid plan to earn the money back right away.

The amount I wanted could've very well been $10, and my wife should've questioned it. After all, what was my plan? How was I going to implement it? Would I expect to spend even more as time went on?

Writing and publishing shouldn't be something you hide from the world. If you're married or working with a partner, have an open conversation about your shared mission and vision as an aspiring author. If you're flying solo, then you'll need to have that conversation with yourself—be your own devil's advocate.

When I first broke into the business officially in March 2014, I spent no money to get going. That's right, zero dollars! The manuscript was atrocious, and the packaging was horrible. Though I had everything working against me on that first book launch, I still made money. With the earnings, I reinvested in my business.

With consistent publishing and diligent writing, my process became more streamlined. Each publication became better, with slicker packaging and more effective editing. As I published each book, I learned more about how to market and promote my book to drive more traffic and increase my sales. By January 2016, I was making enough to pay the bills and have money left over to continue pursuing this writing career.

Fast forward to September 2020 when I released my biggest success yet with *Amazon Keywords for Books*. That book came from months of work and years of business experience. I applied everything I'd learned to that point when I wrote that book. While it's virtually impossible to condense everything I know into one book, I did my best to share what newbie authors should know in that one.

As you start your publishing journey, I highly recommend you stay the course and never give up. When you run into a problem—whether writing blocks or financial limitations—find a way around it. Self-publishing is not easy, but you can simplify the process by sticking to the fundamentals in this book.

In the end, I'm glad my wife shot down my $1,200 request. It was ludicrous for me to ask for that much money. Would I have spent the money wisely? Probably not. We didn't need a garage full of books, and people didn't really want those books anyway. It only made sense that I struck out on my own with nothing more than a willingness to learn the business and become a better writer with every release. With each new book, I got a better sense of what readers truly wanted. Once I had one hit, the subsequent hits came easier.

You'll have a similar journey too. Don't invest what you can't stand to lose. Be ready, willing, and able to not only be a better writer but a better overall self-publisher. Now, go write and publish your next book. Happy publishing!

GET MORE BOOK SALES TODAY!

You wrote the book.

And now it's published.

But you're not getting any sales! What gives?!

Most people would have you believe self-publishing on Amazon is easy. Yet why aren't you seeing the results they claim you should?

A lack of book sales comes down to three culprits:

- Keywords
- Marketing and promotion
- Book reviews

It's time you put all your self-publishing woes to bed and finally increase your book sales for good.

Enter *The Amazon Self-Publisher*.

You'll learn:

- The secrets to keyword research and selection
- Cheap yet effective book promotions
- How to get book reviews the legit way

- Where Amazon Advertising will serve your book best

And hundreds of powerful insights!

You'll love learning all about Amazon self-publishing, because once you discover proven strategies in self-publishing, your life will change for the better.

Order this three-part series in one book now when you visit:

DaleLinks.com/SelfPubBook

A SMALL ASK...

Now that you've finished reading this book, what do you think of what you read? Are there any tips or information you found insightful? What do you think is missing from this book? While you're thinking back on what you read, it'd mean the world to me if you left an honest review on Amazon.

As you probably know, reviews play a part in building relevancy for all products on Amazon. Whether or not you found the information helpful, your candid review will help other customers make an informed purchase.

Also, based on your review, I'll adjust this publication and future editions. That way, you and other indie authors can learn and grow.

Leave a review at DaleLinks.com/ReviewSelfPub.

ABOUT THE AUTHOR

Dale L. Roberts is an award-winning author and video content creator. After publishing over fifty titles and becoming a international bestselling author on Amazon multiple times across various regions, Dale started his YouTube channel, Self-Publishing with Dale. After seven years of producing high-quality content about self-publishing, Dale has cemented his position as the go-to authority in the indie-author community.

Dale currently lives with his wife Kelli and two rescue cats in Columbus, Ohio.

RELEVANT LINKS:

- Website—SelfPublishingWithDale.com
- My Books—DaleLinks.com/MyBooks
- YouTube—YouTube.com/SelfPublishingWithDale
- Discord—DaleLinks.com/Discord
- Twitter—Twitter.com/SelfPubWithDale
- Facebook—Facebook.com/SelfPubWithDale
- Instagram—Instagram.com/SelfPubWithDale

SPECIAL THANKS

I'm forever grateful to you, the reader, for taking time out of your life to read my book. After all, if you don't read this book, then why the heck did I write it? I sincerely hope this book is as fulfilling for you to read as it was for me to write.

Extra big shout-out to Ava Fails and Jeanne De Vita for their help in producing this book. Your assistance was priceless. And, an extra big shout-out to my beta reading team for all the notes and suggestions. I appreciate all of you.

ADDITIONAL RESOURCES

- Amazon Book Sales Calculator for KDP—DaleLinks.com/Calculator
- Audactiy—https://www.audacityteam.org/
- My preferred transcription services
    - Rev—DaleLinks.com/Rev
- *Finish the Damn Book!* by Martin McConnell—DaleLinks.com/FinishTheBook
- My preferred grammar checkers
    - ProWritingAid—DaleLinks.com/ProWritingAid
    - Grammarly—DaleLinks.com/Grammarly
- Alliance of Independent Authors (ALLi)—DaleLinks.com/ALLi
    - ALLi Watchdog List—DaleLinks.com/Watchdog
- *The DIY Publishing Course for Beginners*—DIYPublishing.biz/Free
- My Cover Designers
    - Miblart—DaleLinks.com/Miblart (use coupon code DALE10 for 10% off)
    - GetCovers—DaleLinks.com/GetCovers

ADDITIONAL RESOURCES

- My Curated List of Fiverr Sellers—DaleLinks.com/List
- GIMP Software—GIMP.org
  - Davies Media Design—YouTube Channel covering GIMP tutorials - youtube.com/user/DaviesMediaDesign
  - Logos by Nick—YouTube channel covering GIMP and graphic design tutorials - youtube.com/logosbynick
- Davies Media Design (YouTube)—YouTube.com/c/DaviesMediaDesign
- Logos by Nick (YouTube)—YouTube.com/@LogosByNick
- Pixabay—free image and video resource—Pixabay.com
- 1001 Fonts—free and premium font resource—1001fonts.com
  - Free fonts on 1001 Fonts—1001fonts.com/free-fonts-for-commercial-use.html
- Publishing Distribution
  - Ebook & Print Distribution
    - KDP—kdp.amazon.com
    - IngramSpark—ingramspark.com
    - Draft2Digital—draft2digital.com
  - Audiobook Distribution
    - ACX—acx.com
    - Findaway Voices—findawayvoices.com
    - Audiobooks Unleashed—distribution.audiobooksunleashed.com
    - Lantern Audio—lanternaudio.com
    - Author's Republic—authorsrepublic.com

- Aggregate Ebook, Print Book & Audiobook Distribution
    - PublishDrive—publishdrive.com
    - Streetlib—streetlib.com
- Ebook Distribution
    - Apple—authors.apple.com
    - Kobo—kobo.com/us/en/p/writinglife
    - Barnes & Noble Press—press.barnesandnoble.com
    - Google Play Books—play.google.com/books/publish/u/0/

- Publishing Public Domain Books on Kindle—DaleLinks.com/PublicDomain

- International ISBN Agency—DaleLinks.com/ISBN
- KDP Delivery Fees—DaleLinks.com/KDPDeliveryFees
- KDP Help Page—DaleLinks.com/KDPHelp
- Findaway Voices Help Section—DaleLinks.com/FindawayHelp

- *I Paid 5 Designers on Fiverr To Design the Same Cover*—DaleLinks.com/5Designs

REFERENCES

[i] Carey, B. (24 August 2016). Smartphone speech recognition can write text messages three times faster than human typing. https://news.stanford.edu/2016/08/24/stanford-study-speech-recognition-faster-texting/

[ii] Chesson, D. (24 March 2022). How Many Words Per Page In a Book? Amazon Stats + Survey. https://kindlepreneur.com/words-per-page/

[iii] Reedsy LTD. (27 October 2020) https://blog.reedsy.com/types-of-editing/

[iv] Nortara, K. (7 March 2019) Do You Need a Book Doctor or a Content Editor? https://knliterary.com/book-doctor-or-content-editor/

[v] Audible, Inc. (n.d.) ACX Audio Submission Requirements. https://www.acx.com/help/acx-audio-submission-requirements/201456300

[vi] LaRue, N. (08 October 2018). Why Having Images at 300DPI is so Important. https://www.arka.com/blogs/news/300dpi

[vii] Amazon.com, LLC. (n.d.) Print Options. https://kdp.amazon.com/en_US/help/topic/G201834180

[viii] Haines, D. (19 March 2021). Why The Amazon Books Store Has A Monopoly On Book Sales. https://justpublishingadvice.com/why-do-amazon-sell-more-ebooks-than-other-retailers/

REFERENCES

[ix] Amazon.com, LLC (n.d.). eBook Distribution Rights. https://kdp.amazon.com/en_US/help/topic/G200652410

[x] Amazon.com, LLC (n.d.). Publishing Public Domain Content. https://kdp.amazon.com/en_US/help/topic/G200743940

[xi] Collins, A. (16 November 2021). Psychological Pricing: What Your Prices Really Say to Customers. https://www.shopify.com/blog/psychological-pricing

[xii] Amazon.com, LLC (n.d.). Print Options. https://kdp.amazon.com/en_US/help/topic/G201834180

[xiii] Audible, Inc. (n.d.). How long will my narrated Audiobook be? https://help.acx.com/s/article/how-long-will-my-narrated-audiobook-be

[xiv] Spangler, T. (29 July 2022). Spotify Paid $119 Million for Audiobook Distributor Findaway, Taking on Audible. https://variety.com/2022/digital/news/spotify-findaway-acquisition-price-audiobooks-1235328275/

[xv] Hamilton, J. (24 March 2022). ACX vs Findaway Voices: A Complete Review. https://kindlepreneur.com/acx-vs-findaway-voices/

[xvi] Murphy, D. (10 May 2017). Why I Got Kicked Out of Kindle Unlimited & Lost $50,000 Overnight | Derek Murphy. https://youtu.be/P2J3jJB7bYU?si=mTCwtPLIvW3qO8-z.

[xvii] https://www.copyright.gov/about/fees.html

[xviii] Chesson, D. (19 February 2020). How to Copyright Your Book in Under 7 Minutes. https://youtu.be/HJ5aWu-iKbE?si=C8xCs5CgRFJ7eFU3.

www.ingramcontent.com/pod-product-compliance
Lightning Source LLC
Chambersburg PA
CBHW071710020426
42333CB00017B/2206